THE DAYS GONE BY

AN AUTOBIOGRAPHY OF RICHARD ALTENHOFF SR.

AS WRITTEN BY HIMSELF

authorHOUSE®

AuthorHouse™
1663 Liberty Drive
Bloomington, IN 47403
www.authorhouse.com
Phone: 1-800-839-8640

Published by AuthorHouse   01/16/2013

ISBN: 978-1-4772-9172-6 (sc)
ISBN: 978-1-4772-9171-9 (e)

Library of Congress Control Number: 2012921868

DEDICATION

I PROUDLY DEDICATE THIS BOOK TO MY PARENTS - MY MOTHER, HELEN ALTENHOFF AND FATHER, GEORGE ALTENHOFF SR. WITHOUT THEIR LOVE FOR EACH OTHER THIS STORY COULD NOT HAVE BEEN TOLD AND I WOULDN'T HAVE BEEN ABLE TO WRITE IT. KIND - A MAKES SENSE ANYWAY. THANK YOU MOM AND DAD.

MOM & DAD

PROLOGUE

THIS IS THE STORY OF MY CHILDHOOD GROWING UP IN THE 1950's. I HAVE MANY FOND MEMORIES OF THAT ERA. THE STORIES THAT YOU WILL READ ARE TRUE AND THE PEOPLE HERE ARE REAL, THEIR NAMES HAVE NOT BEEN CHANGED TO PROTECT THE INNOCENT AS THERE ARE NONE..THEY'RE ALL AS GUILTY AS I AM. SOME OF THESE TALES ARE SHORT BECAUSE THE MEMORY IS SHORT BUT I HOPE YOU WILL FIND THEM SOMEWHAT ENTERTAINING ANYWAY. SO, THIS IS THE BEGINNING AS IT WAS THEN.......

THE DAYS GONE BY

CHAPTER ONE

IT ALL STARTS HERE

In May 1946 United States Armed Forces stormed the Federal Penitentiary known as "Alcatraz" in SanFrancisco bay as inmates tried what turned out to be an unsuccessful escape attempt. The inmates held seven guards as hostages in which three were eventually shot and killed. The siege lasted several days an in the end all three would-be escapees were shot and killed.

Also that year, the Montreal Canadiens won their sixth Stanley Cup and boxer Joe Louis, a.k.a. "The Brown Bomber," successfully defended his World Heavyweight Title for the 22nd time.

In November, 1946, Walt Disney released the full length motion picture "THE SONG OF THE SOUTH." One of the brightest and biggest events of the year took place in Oak Park, Illinois on November 24th, when, at 2:55 am. Dr. Anthony Vincenti delivered a scrappy, 7 lb.-13 .oz, 20 1/2 in. charming and delightful, bouncing baby boy. The young newbie would then be named {no! not "Rosemary's Baby"} but Helen's baby, Richard William Altenhoff. A little BS there? Maybe, except for the charming and delightful part of course. Here's a little more for you, it's been said that, "there's no greater joy on this day for Helen and George Altenhoff than the birth of this handsome and lovely angel that now rests in his mothers' arms."

I'm not sure who the person was that said that but, it did wind up spreading far and wide as the years progressed and made the legend grow to what it is today. You know! I'm thinking exactly just what you're thinking, that it might be possible, just possible mind you, that somewhere along the way it might have been me that said it to someone {who might have believed me.} As you read on you'll see that the road to maturity was not an easy one for me. It was a real struggle to grow up and be the wonderful guy that I truly turned out to be. If this BS is getting heavy, just wait, there's more where that came from.

OUR HOUSE

OUR HOUSE

Located at 621 S. 24th Ave., Bellwood, Illinois - rear house. Our house was a little shanty type called a "garage house" so called because it was located in the rear of the main house and was located along the back alley which separated 23rd St. from 24th St. Ours was only one of four located on our block. Everyone else had garages along the alley.

From the time that I was born and until I just started grade school there were actually nine people living there in that tiny house, using only one kitchen, one sink { located in the kitchen} and one bathroom of which had the usual 4-legged tub {no shower, no wash basin} and the toilet, and hot water heater. Everyone who had to wash - up had to use the kitchen sink. There was no linen closet but we did have a medicine cabinet above the toilet. There wasn't any facilities in the upstairs living quarters so the family of four had to use the down stairs facilities as well. The family upstairs consisted of my uncle Stan { called him "junior"} my aunt Eve, my cousins Dorothy and Bernice. My aunt and uncle slept on the north end and my cousins shared a bed on the south end. Only a table with a lamp separated the two rooms.

Being as little as I was, I couldn't realize how tight things really were. My brother and I slept in the small bedroom which had a small window, twin bed that went from wall to wall. We didn't have a closet so we had to hang our clothes on the hooks on the wall at the foot of the bed. Our socks and underwear were in the dresser. When my sister was born her crib was in our room. Our room had the only door except the bathroom and the entrance. My parents used a curtain for their room which was next to the living room. They did have a closet in their room.

THE FAMILY WITHIN: VIOLENCE

My grandmother Antionette Reschik was married to Stanley Reschik and had two sons, Stanley jr. and Joseph. Sometime after Uncle Joe was born, their father died and later my grandmother married William Yorcis. They hand two children, a son Frank and a daughter Helen { my mother}. I never knew my mother's father as he died before I was born.

My Uncle Stan whom I will refer to as "Junior" or Uncle Junior, was a very violent alcoholic. When I say "violent," he actually drew blood from my Aunt Eve and their daughters {my cousins} Dorothy and Bernice. They all lived upstairs as I had mentioned earlier.

9

VIOLENCE{CON'T}

I remember to this day the one incident that scarred me for life. They were arguing upstairs; I was in the kitchen down below with my parents. I remember my father saying "God damn! They're at it again!" You could hear screaming from my Aunt Evelyn and I could hear my cousins crying loudly. My Aunt Eve came down stairs with blood on her face. My mother quickly led me to my room and I was told to stay there. My father and Uncle Junior started yelling at each other. I kind-a blocked it out, as I was so scared. Eventually they were asked to leave and find another place. I can't remember how long afterward.

When my mother died in 1962, my Uncle Junior was stoned out of his mind from the wake to the funeral. I remember at the funeral home my Uncle Junior looked at me and said one thing to me, "I loved her so much." That was the last thing he ever had a chance to say to me and was the last time I ever saw him. I never saw him again and hated him from that day on. When I found out he died, decades later, my Aunt Katie, my Uncle Joe's wife, tried to talk me into driving her to his wake and funeral. I had totally declined, I refused to forgive and forget. I simply said to her, "he could rot in hell."

VIOLENCE CONTINUES: ALCOHOLISM

Alcoholism seemed no stranger to our family. When my father's family move back to Illinois from Sterling, Colorado there were only four kids left out of ten, my father George, his three sisters, Esther {the oldest}, Mary, and Betty, my grandparents Gottlieb and Elizabeth. Aunt Esther married Henry Gorr, they had two children, Art and Norma, Aunt Mary married John Schuppe and they had one child Patricia. Aunt Betty married Gil Troup{her second marriage}. My three Aunts were the kindest most loving Aunts anyone could ever ask for.

My Uncle John was also an extremely violent alcoholic. Beatings against my Aunt Mary and cousin Pat were frequent. My Aunt mary was a very fragile built woman as were her siblings. Uncle John was stocky built so obviously she was no one to be able to fight back.

One day, I think it was a Saturday, my parents dropped me off by cousin Pat's house for awhile. I don't recall if Uncle John was home or not or how long I was there. My Aunt Mary was making me eggs while I was playing on the kitchen floor playing with my toy truck when I heard my Uncle John yell out "Mary! " Pat was in the basement with a neighbor girl. Aunt Mary went into the living room and just as quick they started yelling at each other out loud. I was so scared that I hid under the kitchen table but was able to see what they were doing. I can't remember what they were arguing about, as everything seemed so loud that it was deafening. I saw my uncle grab my Aunt Mary's arm and he proceeded to slap her across the face. She was so fragile looking and stood no chance to fight back. The next thing I remember seeing was him ripping the phone out of the wall and hitting her with it, and actually drawing--blood.

10

VIOLENCE }con't}

Some of the blood splattered on the wall, I was terrified, I couldn't remember if I was even crying or not. All of a sudden my father came crashing through the door and wrestled Uncle John to the floor. My mother grabbed my Aunt Mary. The rest is pretty much blank. Even today when I hear couples arguing, I get a sensation that tells me to run. Something like that you never forget. It does scar you for life.

When my Aunt Mary was dying of cancer, my Uncle John asked mom and dad if she could stay with us for awhile. I remember that she was so thin and frail she could hardly stand up. That was the last time that I saw her alive. My cousin Art came over and drove her and my mom to the hospital where a few days later she died. I recall it was St. Anne's Hospital.

When Uncle John wasn't drinking he was funny and actually fun to be around. People don't forget much. I was the only one who visited him in his home on a regular basis. After mu aunt died no one else would have anything to do with him.

There's nothing worse than having a young child, not yet school age, to see and hear all this anger, hate and violence all at one time being shed against one person. Real blood, real life--it was terrifying to experience.

CHAPTER TWO

GROWING UP--

MY WAY

CHAPTER TWO

GROWING UP...MY WAY
  It doesn't matter what decade you grew up in because the memories of that time are very precious. The good things and the bad things are all a part of what and who we are today. Our experiences back then had set the mold of today.
  I was lucky to grow up in the 1950's. In our house at least, kids were "seen, not heard," and that meant, for example, at the dinner table, only the parents did the talking and us kids had to be silent unless we were spoken to directly. When you put food on your plate you were expected to eat everything that was put there, and no such thing as "I'm finished, can I go now.?" You sat there until you finished everything. If you didn't like what Mom cooked, you didn't have to eat, but you were not allowed to raid the refrigerator to satisfy your hunger.
  We had to keep ourselves occupied at whatever we came up with to be out of the way until bed time. Our parents, aunts, uncles and grandparents did not play with us as they do today or when I was a father, back then it was kids on kids and adults with adults. To find something to do to occupy our time we generally had to be creative because at Christmas time we each got only one toy and that had to last because there was no such thing as "getting a new one" whether it was lost, broken, or stolen. Our last responsibility as a child was just before bed time when we would gather around the TV set to not only watch but to take turns turning the TV dial to switch channels of which sometimes we would argue over whose turn it was to do it. We had to watch whatever our parents wanted to watch or find something else to do before going to bed. We could only watch if our homework was done and our parents were satisfied that it was indeed, "done."
  After school or on weekends we could watch what we wanted before dinner. Some of our favorite TV shows were, ELMER THE ELEPHANT, HOWDY DOODY, SUSANS' SHOW, GARFIELD GOOSE, ROOTIE KAZOOTY and many others.
  Our part of town was small as far as the number of kids to play with. Most were either my brothers' age or girls, so I was pretty much forced to be creative or be bored. We had six open fields within a two - block radius of our house. I was very much satisfied to be creative because then I could do whatever I wanted to do and not be bossed around so I could be called a "loner." I liked to call these fields "The Wilderness." I was my own version of Davy Crockett. The only difference was that my wilderness did not have big game such as deer, bear and stuff like that. In the upcoming episodes you'll meet some of the other most savagest critters known to man and you'll quickly learn that I turned out to be the most savage of them all and how I turned some of them into table meat.

BEE CAREFUL

One early morning as I awoke, I decided to play a trick on my mother. I was not yet of school age but was pretty smart. While she was doing the ironing in the kitchen I quickly jumped out of my bed and covered my pillow to make her think that I was still asleep. I then opened the side door of my dresser and was small enough and able to squeeze in and partially close the door. I must have dozed off a bit. When she came in my room and opened the dresser door she was startled enough to drop the clothes on the floor. She gently grabbed my arm and with gentle force she pulled me out and softly, but sternly, told me not to do it again. That was MOM, I miss her a lot.

I then got dressed then had my daily dose of Quaker Oats oatmeal, buttered bread topped with cinnamon and coffee to dunk it in, {the bread, not the oatmeal}. After breakfast i was ready to tackle the wilderness that lay out there before me.

On this particular morning I decided to go to the field that lay across the street behind those houses and across their alley. I always carried a stick for protection because I knew this field had skunks, mice, snakes and bees. Well, on this trip I ran across a huge beehive. Must have been thousands of honeybees. I made my way back home to think about my next move and carefully plan my strategy as to how to conquer these vicious critters.

I was used to catching them in a jar one by one, sometimes flower and all. I would do that by waiting for them to land on the flower then cautiously make my move, reach out, holding the cover and jar with the flower in between them. When the bee landed then I would pull the cover and jar together with lightning speed thus capturing this stinging menace. One time I had as many as three bees in one jar without ever being stung. If you think that was easy then I urge you to give it a try. You're talking to the master bee catcher. If it's any consolation to you animal activists out there, the jar cover had holes in it so they could breathe, but in most cases, they would be dead by morning anyway. They did a lot of buzzing in there though before they croaked. It was kinda fun to hear their desperate, angry buzzing for help. I liked the echo sound coming from the jar. I did, however, miss a couple of times too, but as usual, I walked away unscathed..Experience pays.

Being the skillful, crafty hunter that I was I knew that this hive was going to be a challenge. This was a hive, not a flower of easy pickings. A jar was definitely out of the question. this was my plan that was well laid out.

I would find a rock big enough to crush the hive and kill as many as possible then run like the wind. I figured that the escapees would fly off to find another nest. Sounded reasonable at the time. After a few minutes of searching I found a rock that I thought was big enough and walked toward the hive and got close enough to "Let 'er fly." Once the rock was thrown I had to run as fast as lightning. They were gonna bee pissed. I figured I'd be far enough away before they ever knew what hit 'em. Turned out they were quite a bit smarter than I was. I knew that I had hit the hive pretty good, simple enough, exactly where, I knew not. I heard the thud then took off with blinding speed. As I crossed the alley I could feel the piercing stingers penetrating my upper back. I screamed for help as loud as I could. Our neighbor "big John" ran out of his house and caught up with me. He started brushing them off my back and neck, then guided me home. I wound up with five stings. My mother pulled them out with tweezers then put some salve on the wounds.

The next day I built up enough nerve to go back and check on the damage, with extreme caution of course. When I got there I could see the rock that I had tossed and noticed what a well-placed shot I had made. There were many dead, none wounded, the rest escaped and moved on. I should have joined the Air Force to fly on bombing raids. It was safer than using a jar although the area looked like a bee holocaust.

On occasion I would also catch spiders with a jar then capture a bee or two just to see what happens--usually nothing. Since I came out of this with only five stings, I would have to say that, indeed, I was victorious over these little varmints.

GREAT WHITE HUNTER: BIGGER PREY

Since I put a dent into the bee population, I figured it was time to move onto bigger prey, something with more of a challenge and harder to catch. I always was {and still am] ready for any challenge. This time it would be snakes and mice. Oh, come on! they're bigger than bees.

Today I would carry my stick and travel down the alley and head south to the "Big field" which was three blocks long stretching from 25th Ave. west to east 22nd St. Usually I would go in the morning because snakes would lay out in the sun to warm their bodies. When I would locate one I would go behind it and gently grab it by the tail and then lift it up gently so as not to scare it. While it would squirm a bit, I would lay it down and pin it's head down with my forked stick, then take out my knife and cut off it's head. Later in life I would hunt rattlesnakes in Texas, but that story maybe in a possible book two, I would catch them the same way.

One morning my aunt, who lived in the big house in front, came to me all shaken up. She asked me if I could get rid of the snake in the basement on the ledge between the window and the oil drum. I told her that "I'll see what I could do." I went down to the basement, walked around the drum and could see that the snake was still there on the ledge. Of course I had my trusty snake catching stick. The snake kind of put himself in a bad position because there was no escape route for him, he had to come in my direction from the floor. I couldn't reach him to be able to grab him. I had my stick ready to make my move. I reached in with my stick and kinda pinned him. As he stretched out I then grabbed his tail and had to quickly pull him out. After I did so, I dropped my stick, took my right hand and moved down his body to where I could hold him by his neck and carry him outside to the alley where I then proceeded to pull the snake apart and throw the body parts into the small field across the alley. Guaranteed he was dead.

A little extreme perhaps but when someone asks me to do a job..I do it...my way and it gets done one way or the other. My aunt was grateful. She gave me a shiny new quarter to buy an ice cream bar. Thanks to me, snakes were in short supply around our block. Maybe a little gross at times but I'm sure of this: I'll never have my own TV show on Animal Planet.

THE LEGEND GROWS: WHACK JOB

In this portion of chapter two, you will not only know just what a "Whack Job" is but you will learn here, the fine art of "Whacking," of which I have invented and perfected.

Well! This time I felt that I was through with small stuff, The challenge had to be bigger; you know the saying that goes The bigger they are, the harder they fall." Well this is it folks. A prey that has four feet and can out run anything, at least in my neighborhood. when these critters met up with me they soon realized that I could, and have, out run a lightning bolt. You might not have guessed the name of this beast by now, so, I will tell you. He is "Mr. Cottontail." Yes! The rabbit. I have turned many of these into table meat, but this particular one was my greatest challenge up to that point. This varmint would pillage gardens and flower beds and I was up to the task of getting rid of them.

I remember this as if it were yesterday. It was Saturday, somewhat snowy but cloudy. Carrying my gunnysack and my Louisville Slugger 34 inch Monte Irvine baseball bat, I started my block and a half walk to the "big field." Lots of rabbits, pheasants. My concern today--rabbits. Plenty of snow on the ground made it easy to be quiet. I wasn't too far in when I spooked my prey.

16

I was a little spooked myself. He shot out like a cannonball and started running to safety. I would have said that he was "heading for the hills' but there wasn't any. The field was flat and he had nowhere to hide. I lost sight of him so I decided to follow his tracks. I did so for a few minutes and I noticed that his tracks came to an end. "Weird," I thought, he had to be somewhere. I remembered that when they're scared and have no place to go, they burrow themselves into the snow. Smart! I'm a little smarter though.

I got down on my knees and started to dig and after a short time when I came across a little ball of brown fur. I was always told by certain species of humans of the opposite sex that I was always good with my hands. Anyway, I put down my stuff and quickly grabbed this little fur ball which turned out to be quite beefy, almost the size of a cat. He was certainly more than a couple of hands full. I brought him up and he was squirming all over the place--I almost lost control of him. I was able to firmly grip his hind legs and hold him up with his head facing the ground.

The "Whack job" is now going to take place. As I held him I had to reach down for my Louisville Slugger 34in. Monte Irvin special baseball bat. I had to make sure that the "Trademark" on the bat was facing away from the contact point so as not to break the bat. The bat cost me $4.00 at the time. I had to "choke up" on the bat { holding the bat a little higher from the bottom knob} which gives you more power. I took a quick swing and hit the rabbit behind the neck so as to kill him quickly. But this time I didn't hit him hard enough and had to whack him again with a little more force. I connected quite well with the second swing and just that quick I knew he was dead. How did I know for sure? Simple-he stopped squirming and his eyes were bulging out and his tongue was hanging out. I threw him in my gunny sac and went home. Because my mother had been preparing the evening meal, this catch was an appetizer.

Now you know just what a "whack job" is. As always, I came out on top again. I'm just no match for any size critters. It's illegal to kill elephants and alligators.

THE TRUTH BE TOLD
The big bear hunt: May 4, 1977

Although this story didn't take place during my childhood I am including it here because the record of this event must be set straight once and for all-as it has been twisted and misconstrued a few times. This is a perfect place to tell it like it actually was and how it really happened. To make the story short and to the point, I am eliminating the events that led to this Alaskan adventure by going right into the hunt.

Kodiak Island, Alaska--May 4, 1977. This was the 8th day of my ten- day fair chase hunt. When I say "fair chase" it simply means that we spot bears by boat using binoculars, when we find one we go to shore then hunt them down as baiting is not allowed.

My guides on this hunt were my head guide, Wayne Hans who has 25 yrs. of guiding experience and his assistant, an Eskimo, Daniel Boone Reed. On this day Wayne and I spotted this huge bear. Wayne estimated it to be at least 12 ft. high when standing, and roughly 2000 pounds. He said that it was it was the biggest bear he'd ever seen in all his years of guiding or hunting. Outside of an elephant, it was also the biggest animal I had ever seen.

The bear was on an incline about 30 yards above us. We were down in the thick alder brush without having a good shot at him. Not enough clearance to hit him. Had we tried to shoot and missed I wouldn't have been around to write this book and my kids would have grown up without a father. No fiction here. We would have been a nice hearty meal for him. As we sat quietly the huge bear made a loud grunting sound as he looked down at us the turned around and ran off. It was then we decided to split up, go up the hill and track him down. Wayne headed north and I headed south.

After what seemed like only a few minutes I heard Wayne yell, "Rich, he's coming your way!" With my gun ready I looked to my right and saw him coming my way. All in an instant, I raised my rifle, quickly shot and I know for a fact that I missed. The bear turned aside from me and I fired again. No time to aim. I know that I hit him this time because he paused for a quick second. He was about 25 yards from me {estimate}. I know he was pretty close. I shot again, this time knocking this very angry animal, down. I was going to shoot again but my gun jammed. The bear stood up, bleeding and waving his huge paws. The only thing I could do now was to drop my rifle, pull out my Bowie knife and take a football type run at him. With my left forearm out in a blocking position, my knife drawn, I ran full speed right into him, knocked him off balance and within seconds I felt my knife penetrate his body somewhere. We both rolled down the 20 ft. embankment to the edge of the small creek. Everything happened so fast, though it sounds like minutes, it was like my head was spinning all over the place, a Twilight Zone moment. During the tumble I felt a little sting on my left leg and lower back. I looked to my left and saw the bear's tongue hanging out. I knew he was dead. I felt pretty groggy myself. I heard Wayne call out"Rich! Where are you?" I yelled back "Down here Wayne." Wayne picked up my rifle and came down to help me.

Big Bear hunt {con't}

With my shirt all bloody and my leg and back bleeding some, I waded into the creek to clean up. The creek was only about 6 in. deep and about 5 ft. wide but icy cold. After I cleaned up, we cut the bear open so the predators wouldn't damage the fur. We had to mark the spot then leave for camp because it was getting too dark to skin it so we had to leave it overnight, besides the big male bear was still around somewhere.

The next day, Wayne, and assistant guide, Al, and I went back to the spot that I had marked with my white T-shirt the night before, to skin the bear. while the skinning was going on, Wayne noticed something protruding from the bear's heart. It turned out to be my bullet. The bullet almost went right through her {it was determined that the bear was female}. I shot so fast without trying to aim, because there was no time to do that. I knew that she was hit but I couldn't tell where. It had to be mine because Wayne wasn't there to even take a shot and it was confirmed by him that it was my bullet. My other shot went through her left side underbelly and exited the other side. The bullet went through both of her lungs.

Before I left for home, Wayne and Daniel told me that, to date, was one of the most exciting hunts they've ever guided. I had a rug made of the bear and the bullet is incased in plastic.

LUCKY SHOT: THE LAST HUNT

I had decided not to do a Book 2 so I want to squeeze this one story in anyway.

One more hunting story. To this day it was my last hunt, a successful hunt even though I didn't get the critter I was really after. This one concerns the coonskin hat that's been hanging in my cabin in Wisconsin and now hang here in my Crystal Lake home. I have been asked about it several times and never had an appropriate time to tell it in it's entirety so I decided to enter it here in this chapter of my book.

Actually, this took place just a short time after the big bear hunt. I'm not sure of the year. I was down in East Tennessee with my buddy "Spider" Higgins, who was born in that neck of the woods. You can probably guess where his nickname from. He had a huge pet tarantula and was one of those spider lovers. For me, they give me the creeps. I'd rather be with rattlesnakes and alligators than any kind of spiders. To each his own I guess.

I was carrying my .45 caliber flintlock rifle on this trip and as a backup gun I carried my holstered .45 caliber Buntline Special pistol with my trusty, bear killing Bowie knife on my left side. Spider believed in "One shot kill" so he carried a 30.06 rifle.

On our third day out it was starting to get late and we were ready to call it a day when we heard this funny noise coming from a nearby tree. We figured it to be either a squirrel or a raccoon. We came upon the right tree and noticed two raccoons side by side. Spider didn't want to shoot them because had he used his gun he would have blown them to pieces. My rifle was already loaded and ready. The raccoons were probably mating or getting ready to mate. Normally they don't hang out that close together.

I pulled my hammer back and slowly took aim as Spider stood motionless. I pulled the trigger and my rifle let out a big puff of smoke. After the smoke had cleared Spider and I stood in amazement, as we now saw two raccoons lying on the ground. One of them wasn't quite dead so I used my Buntline Special to finish him off. Only one shot fired and two coons down. When we knelt down to look at them we noticed that one of them had his left eye shot out and was bleeding profusely. The other was shot between the eyes. What made this truly amazing was that I was actually aiming for his heart. Anyway, we figured out that when I cocked my rifle, the raccoon in the back moved over to his right to hide behind the other. When I pulled the trigger both of them were hit. Pretty decent shooting considering I was aiming for the heart. Spider and I decided to make coonskin caps out of them. His friend was a taxidermist and he made them for us.

Several months later I received mine. Spider kept the one with one eye. So, if you're ever in southeast Tennessee and see a man wearing a one-eyed coonskin cap ..it could be Spider Higgins.

BB GUN: LAST SHOT

Back to the child hood days. This episode is not "The Christmas Story" about shooting my eye out or anything like that. My father wasn't concerned about me shooting my eye out, he was more concerned about me shooting someone. I did have thick glasses, though.

One early evening, I was walking back home from the park and in the alley, standing all by itself against the Landers' garage, next to the garbage cans was a BB gun lever action rifle. I figured it must have been thrown out otherwise it wouldn't have been there, right? I felt that it was my duty to rescue this poor thing, so I did what any normal boy would have done, I took it to safety, meaning, I brought it home and hid it in the porch closet in the far corner so my father wouldn't see it. I didn't want to see this beauty destroyed and sent to the landfill, gone forever.

It was summertime, so my father had no real reason to use the closet as it was used to hang our coats and had a basket of toys on the floor. The next day I went to the Bell-May store and bought two packs of BB's as they were ten-cents per pack. When I got home I was ready to load the gun and have some fun. I went out to the front yard and noticed a squirrel next to the tree. I figured I'd give him something to remember. My first shot hit him in the ass and he scampered up the tree. I decided to let him be. I then saw a Robin by the front bushes along the sidewalk. I took aim and shot him in the wing. All he could do was hop around because he couldn't fly. I shot him a few more times to put him out of his misery and he then fell dead as a doornail. The neighbor lady came out and yelled at me to stop. After killing one more and wounding another I had to quit for now. I headed for the big field to finish off my BB's by killing one snake and two mice. It was getting late so I decided to head home before my father got home.

When I got home, mom was cooking dinner and I quickly stuffed the rifle deep into it's hiding place in the closet. After dinner my father went into the living room to read the paper, "The Chicago Sun-Times." He then called out to me "Richie! When you're done eating, come in here. I want to talk to you." When I finished my dinner I went to the living room and sat in the big chair. He then asked me "Where's your BB gun? Stunned and now trembling I could almost feel the "belt." If that happens I knew I wouldn't be sitting anymore anytime soon. It was obvious to me that nosey old snitch with four eyes next door had ratted on me. I was told to "Get it right now!" I went to retrieve it and all the while I kept thinking of my poor butt. I gave it to him and was told to "Sit down." I figured this was going to be the last time that my butt was going to feel comfort for quite a while. What happened next was a total surprising shock. He asked me where I got it, I told him, and then he took out the BB holder from the barrel the bent it over his knee. My mind was in high gear now; "Whack time, here it comes," Then in a loud voice he said, "I told you to never play with a BB Gun. If someone would have called the police, you'd be in jail right now." "Jail?" I thought. "Ball and chain, striped pajamas, handcuffs, steel bars?" I couldn't stand the thought of it. With a few tears running down my face I told him "It'll never happen again."

I walked around for awhile thinking that I was off the hook, close call, butt saved, never again, I never touched it again and don't remember what happened to it.

CHAPTER THREE

TONY & ME

TONY AND ME

Tony was not related to anyone in the family but a great friend to anyone who knew him. I knew nothing of his background except that he had a son and an older brother Joe who everyone called "old Joe." I can only tell you about Tony from my own experiences with him and the great joy this man brought to me in the few short years that I knew him. To me he was the kind of grandfather that my own wasn't.

Tony lived alone in a shanty much like ours but a little smaller and did not have an upstairs. He was very kind, generous, and very funny. No disrespect to him but he could make you laugh just by looking at him. He had a heart made of pure gold. He didn't have any possessions to speak of, except his 49' Plymouth and his fishing stuff. He had basic stuff such as a few clothes, a cot to sleep on, old fashioned stove and refrigerator, table and a couple of chairs. Oh, just one more thing, he loved his "Vino" as he called it, I think it was whiskey.

Tony could drink anyone under the table; he was never without. He was a very happy-go-lucky kind of alcoholic. Never, ever violent or sarcastic to anyone. Now that I'm older I can really see the sadness on his face and unhappy he really was.

My father always told me that Tony worshiped me and wished that I was his son, a type of son that he wished his own could have been. I get emotional when I think that a person I love would love me that much. It's a tremendous feeling. When Tony would come by, it was only me that he allowed to sit on his lap and hold his drink. The photo shows you that. It's the only known photo of him and it is most dear to my heart.

Tony gave me my first fishing pole. After letting me use it on so many trips, he finally gave it to me. It was a two part bamboo. The top half was black and the bottom half was a lighter color like original bamboo. It had a red cork bobber and black thread line. He knew how much I liked it and I remember vividly that when we came home from fishing, he got out of the car, grabbed the pole and told me to put in the house. "It's yours to keep," he said to me with that monstrous grin. Words can't say enough of how happy I was that, not only did I have my very first fishing pole, but Tony gave it to me. I used it as a second pole for many years after he died.

Most of the time when it was time to go fishing, our party consisted of me, our neighbor Kenny, and Grandma Yorcis- my mother's mother. Us boys would sit in the back seat; Tony and Gramma would sit in the front. When we were all in the car Tony would yell out loud, "Let's get the fish boys, Lets get the fish!"

On the way to our fishing spot which was either Warrenville or Fullersburg, Tony and Gramma would be talking and laughing and on several occasions we could see Gramma pushing Tony's hand aside and she'd say, "Stop it! Not now."We were too young then to know just what was going on. We started to laugh but didn't know what we were laughing at. In todays terminology you would say that "Tony was copping a feel " or "Tony was trying to get in her pants." You older folks know what I mean. As I see it now, Tony was steering the car with his left hand and using his right to steer Gramma in another direction.

When we would safely arrive to our destination along the river Tony would tell us boys to "Go to the bridge and cross the river there and find a spot there." After settling in on the other side we could see that Tony and Gramma had suddenly disappeared for awhile. We never really saw Tony catch any fish but, you can bet he had some action on his pole, if you know what I mean, and I'm sure some of you older folks know.

A weekly ritual for me came on Sundays after church. Tony would pay 50 cents a week to mop his floors and feed his rooster, which he kept in his yard. I would always try to finish fast so I could get my shiny new quarters to spend any way that I wanted. One Sunday after I finished my chores Tony said to me " I don't have 50 cents this time." My mind was racing in frenzy. "No money to spend!" I thought. Then Tony told me to come by the table. He grabbed something, patted me on the head and said, "My boy," he always called me his boy, "Take this instead." It was a real one- dollar bill, a whole dollar, just for me. "Two 50 cents," I thought. He hugged me, smiled and said, "Thank you, my boy." He always called me his boy. I thanked him again too.

One cold February Sunday morning I was getting ready to go by Tony's and my father then came home and saw me getting ready. He told me that I couldn't go to Tony's today, he was sick and in the hospital. I asked my father "What's wrong with Tony?" He simply said, "I don't know." I remember feeling pretty scared by now. I got my coat on and walked over to his house anyway. When I arrived, the rooster was gone, and Tony's door was locked. A streak of fear and loneliness set in real fast. I started to cry a little on my way home.

TONY AND ME {con't}

Two days had passed and still no word about my best friend Tony. Tuesday morning rolled around and my mother did her usual thing, she opened our bedroom door and told my brother and I to "Get up and get dressed for school." My brother was always the first one up. Then it was my turn. My mother came back in, looked at me with sad eyes and said, "Tony died this morning." I'll never forget that. I was devastated. She hugged me then softly said, "Get up and get ready for school." I was heartbroken. I knew then that I was never going to see him again. It's hard to write this and feel all this again even now. No one to this day has ever touched my life the way Tony did.

It was now time for the wake and funeral. When we arrived at the funeral home this cold Thursday morning, I slowly walked through the door. From a short distance I could see Tony in his casket. He was wearing a gray suit; his gray hair was neatly combed back. I could see him more clearly as I got closer. He had his usual small grin from the left side of his face. Lastly, Tony wore a tie today. I smiled at him, touched his cold hand. I didn't know if it was okay to cry or not--no one else did, so I didn't. I had to hold back. Finally they closed his blue cloth covered casket. He was gone forever, never will I see him again. Only a small hand full of people were there to say good-bye to him.

After we left the cemetery a few people came over to our house for brunch. I never felt more alone. I wanted to cry so badly. I grabbed my record player and brought it upstairs and played Duane Eddy's new recording "The Lonely One." My tears started flowing down like Niagara Falls. I think of Tony every time I play that even today 2011.

A couple of days later I came into the house from playing and my father was standing in the porch. Next to the bathroom against the wall was Tony's fishing stuff. My dad said, "Tony wanted you to have it." His favorite fishing rod and tackle box. I picked up his pole and held it for awhile. I then realized how much I really missed him and still do today. I used his stuff for quite a few years before age took over and the pole broke while catching a carp. Both poles broke by way of the carp. I wish I could hear him say one more time, "Let's get the fish boys! Let's get the fish."

CHAPTER FOUR
SCHOOL DAZE 1953-1960

ME AGE 6 - 1st GRADE

ST SIMEON SCHOOL--ROOM 101 BELOW

CHAPTER FOUR
School Daze: Nightmare on Bohland Ave.

All good things must end someday. The freedom trail ends with the first day of school. Yes! school, for the next twelve years at least. Twelve years of mayhem, at least for me. For most of the rest this book you'll learn what a catholic school is really like. For those eight years it was hell on wheels, as you will learn, especially St. Simeon in Bellwood. It was worse than a maximum-security prison. After reading this perhaps you too will wonder where these psycho nuns got the idea that they were married to God. I believe in God totally without question so I firmly believe these nuns couldn't have been married to him, they were born from Satan or they escaped from the nut house and were disguised as nuns.

My nightmare started from day one, my very first day of school ever, before I even got there. I told my mother that I wasn't going to school. All that crying and screaming didn't do a lick of good. My mother sternly said I was going whether I liked it or not and that was that. In my own mind, no one was going to take away my freedom, not without a fight. My mother knew that this was not going to be an easy chore, so she enlisted the neighbor lady to help out. It takes more than one to handle this stubborn mule. EEEEHAW.

The school wasn't more than a five-minute ride from our house so we were there in a jiffy. When we rounded the last corner and the school was now in full view, my panic started to kick in; the tension mounted. I had to find a way out and quick. My mother parked the car and my emotion kicked in to high gear, I started crying and screaming again. My mother opened the door, reached in, and grabbed my arm to pull me out. When I got far enough out, our neighbor Florence grabbed my other arm and the dragging of me started in high gear. I tried to pull away but to no avail. I figured sooner or later they would get tired and give up and take me home. Not my mother; she was determined to get me there even if I was in pieces, if that's what it took. I would rather have had the belt..I think. We got inside finally and when I saw Sister Leonardo standing outside room 101 waiting for me, I really freaked out. To me, she stood as tall as a telephone pole. All dressed in black with a wide white collar--really scared the turds out of me. There was no way I was going near her. She smiled and motioned with her finger to come up and that "Everything is all right." "Not for me," I thought. I was crying and screaming "I don't want to go there!" It did absolutely no good. After pulling me upstairs, I finally succumbed, the battle was over, lost forever, but I stated to everyone "I'm not going to like it." Now when I think about it, my mother had to be very embarrassed, then had to admit that I was her kid. I was given a seat next to Susan Peck, my very first friend, kinda cute too. Wasn't so bad after all. She had a way to calm me down.

SCHOOL DAZE FIRST GRADE
SUSAN PECK - FIRST FRIEND

Up to now I was always on my own and doing whatever I wanted, whenever I wanted--my own boss. School was different, I had a lot more kids around me now and they were all my age. Up to now the only girls I knew were my sister and a couple of her friends. Now there were all kinds, long - haired ones, short-haired ones, cute one and ugly ones. Something new. It took a little while but I finally met some boys I could play with, like Johnny Oats who was my first buddy. Johnny and I had something in common: we both liked to shoot marbles, and soon we started playing some games and some of the other boys joined us.

Marbles was a simple game to play. You started out by digging a hole in the ground by digging our shoe heel into the dirt and spinning around till we had our hole then brushed away the excess dirt. This hole was called "the pot.} If your marble landed in there you were given a free shot to shoot at anyone's marble of your choice. If you hit someone's marble- you took it, kept it, and he was out of the game. You would shoot by making a semi fist with your thumb under your first finger and your marble resting on your first finger in front of your thumb. Your hand had to be on the ground and firm. Then you would release the marble by springing your thumb forward to release the marble. Your hand could not move forward. That was called "Fudging" and you would lose a turn. The idea was to win everyone's marbles. Sometimes I'd win everyone's marbles and walk away with a bag full, sometimes I'd lose my marbles. I know what you're going to say.

Girls didn't play marbles; they were into girl stuff like hopscotch, jump rope, or dodgeball. Susan was pretty good at everything---she was talented and very smart.

As long as we're on the subject of Susan Peck, I'll tell you of a little encounter I had with her at our first grade spring picnic{ too young for other encounters }. It was a nice warm, sunny spring day and our class went to nearby Memorial Park for the picnic. The park was big and had lots of picnic tables and three cannons from World War Two. I was feeling a little feisty on this day, so I decided to play a little trick on Susan. I was sitting next to her while she was opening her goodie bag and an apple rolled out. I grabbed her apple, ran over to the big cannon that was closest to the lagoon, stuck the apple as far down the barrel as my hand could reach, then I sat on top of the barrel, laughing. I saw Susan talking to Sister Leonardo and they were looking at me. I kinda thought I might be in some trouble. They didn't think for a minute that it was so funny. Sister called me over, yelled at me, and made me sit next to her the rest of the day.

Johnny, Susan and I remained friends until after graduation, then I never saw them again.

Summer Vacation: Home Sweet Home

With my first year of school finally over, it was time to get back to normal {whatever that is}, hunting, swimming, hopping freight trains, etc.

Now that I mention it, you know there's something about trains that fascinates young boys. I'm not exactly sure what it is-- power, size, noise, I don't know. One thing for me is that I always wondered what a real Hobo looked like in person.

Once in awhile I'd hop on the ladder of a moving boxcar by the big field and hang on till it got to 22 nd street, then jump off. I really didn't realize how dangerous it was, but it was fun. A couple of times we were lucky enough to see an actual steam locomotive come by and we'd watch it go to the railroad yards. They soon would be replaced by diesel ones of today.

Along Addison Creek, about two blocks from my house, trains would always run north and south to and from the Proviso yards, as they still do today. Well below the tracks down the hill I had a clearing that I had cut out of the trees and brush so I could go and sit and wait for Hobos. It was my personal getaway. I had an old tree stump that I used for a chair and then sometimes I would have a little fire and roast marshmallows or green apples--a quiet place to listen to the trains roll by...Clickety-clack, clickety-clack.

Little Runaway:

It was a late Sunday afternoon, I had an argument with my father and once and for all I felt that I had had enough, so I took some matches and a few apples from the fridge and decided that I was going to runaway. Maybe I would hop a freight train and go wherever it takes me. My first place I always run to is my spot by the creek. I started my fire to keep warm, then roasted an apple to satisfy my hunger. Waiting for the train, I figured I'd show my ol' man a thing or two. It started getting a little cooler, and then I realized that I hadn't any money, no water, and no jacket. When I started to think about things, I remembered that the TV show "Maverick" was coming on pretty soon. I didn't want to miss that. Maybe things weren't so bad after all. Home sweet home. As of 1998 my spot was still there, vacant, and my stump chair was badly decayed.

Danger:

Trains, bone chilling adventure and the unknown also fascinate most boys my age growing up in the 1950's, as shown in the story you are about to read next.

Danger {con't}

I was in the big field on this day enjoying the vastness of this wide-open wilderness when A serious thought came into my mind. "What would it be like to see a real train wreck?" Putting a penny or a nickel on the tracks didn't do anything but get flattened. I ran out of pennies and didn't want to use my spending money anymore. I had to think of something more practical. In an instant I said to myself, "self! There it is," pointing at the switch that changes directions of the train to another track. Lifting that big lever was very hard because of my size. It took me about ten minutes but I did it. Now all I had to do was wait for a train. Almost an hour went by when I was feeling tired of waiting. Just as I got ready to leave I heard a freight coming. I jumped into the ditch to wait for the action. After a few minutes I realized that someone could get killed, but it was too late, the train kept coming. After a while the train passed me by. I was shocked that nothing happened. I couldn't figure it out After the train completely passed, I went back to the switch. It was still in the position that I placed it. I flipped it back to where it was and noticed that the track didn't change. It was disconnected. Close call for me. I never tried anything like that again. I couldn't live with myself knowing someone could have died. not a funny game to play.

SCHOOL DAZE FIRST GRADE
NOTORIOUS ROOM 101

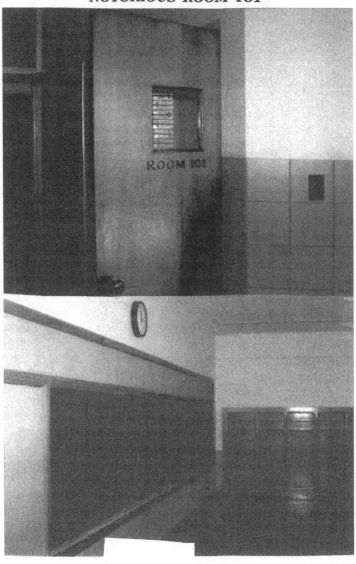

CHAPTER FIVE

FIRE STARTER

CHAPTER FIVE - FIRE STARTER

A GOOD MATCH:

My high spirited moods sometimes could be quite costly,
especially when I possess a book of matches. I have
been known to make some pretty risky chances.

M first chance came one late Saturday when my parents
and some neighbors were in the yard for a long "BS"
session. I really didn't really feel like sitting around to a
nothing gab fest so I decided to take a nice long walk
to the big field and mosey around. I enjoyed moseying when
bored. In my pocket, as usual, was a book of matches. This
time while moseying, I noticed a couple of boxcars with the
doors open, so I went over to one and climbed aboard { I
checked it out for hobo's first as I did not want to be
kidnapped and be a statistic}. I got bored just sitting there so
I casually lit some matches and flipped them into the boxcar.
A short time later I began to smell smoke. I looked back and
saw that the straw had caught fire. I quickly jumped off and
high-tailed it back home. I got back to the yard huffing and
puffing. I was asked where I had been and I answered, "I ran
around the block." Within minutes fire engines started to
come our way down 25th Ave. You could see the black smoke
from our yard. I ran down to the corner and could see the
whole boxcar on fire. I thought my heart was going to pop
right out of my throat. I walked around the block and threw
the matches away so nobody could accuse me of such a
dastardly deed. Right away I thought to myself, "Self! - no
more playing with matches." Sometimes, "you just don't
learn, do ya?"

HOLY SMOKES!

A few friends of mine, Mike Kodwecka, the twin brothers-
Warren and Jimmy Johnson and I had gone to the big field
and dug a trench about 20 ft. long and about 4 ft. wide with a
circular ending so we could gather around and pow wow
once in a while. We covered the floor with a lot of straw and
brush so we could sit and not get to dirty. We stole some
metal sheathing from the coal yard that they weren't using.
We then would cover that with brush so as to hide our
hideout. We obviously had to crawl to get to our circle. We
all brought flashlights. Mike bright some girly magazines
that showed women showing their naked breasts. It was the
first time some of us had ever seen them {the books and the
breasts}. We were all excited about this but weren't sure
why; we weren't old enough to do anything about it yet. The
first time actually seeing nipples and wondering what it
would be like to touch them. After all the looking, laughing,
and joking, we decided to call it a night and meet next
weekend.

HOLY SMOKES {CON'T}

I went there on my own a couple of days later to be by myself. It was getting a little chilly so I gathered around a small pile of brush to make a little fire to keep warm. When I started the fire, I was quickly getting overcome by smoke.

I forgot one important thing....there was no way to vent out the smoke. I quickly crawled out backwards to get precious air. In panic, before getting out, I put more brush in thinking it would smother the fire. No chance. I hightailed it home. Next thing I knew the fire department from Bellwood, Maywood and Broadview were trying to put out this tremendous blaze.

The next day I went back to the field and saw nothing but blackened soil and a few crispy critters and rabbit carcasses. This wasn't the first time that I had burnt it down, but it was the last time. I went home thinking, "now that my hunting ground was gone forever, I would have to do something else." I did! Read on.

ROASTED SQUIRRELS

It was now October, late afternoon and my parents had just brought home our brand spanking new, pushbutton automatic 1959 Nash Rambler American by trading in our old 1952 Plymouth, the famous car that my sister Dianna {aka "Toots"} fell out of. That's another story for later. Everyone had Fords or Chevys. We had a plymouth, as I called it. It was a solid, safe car, but everyone else drove Fords or Chevys.

Back then the new model cars for the next year were available by mid October of the previous year. Getting back to whatever I was writing about...So my parents had the newest car on the block, a Rambler, everyone else still had Fords and Chevy's.

My dad always parked in the alley next to the yard. On the other side of the alley was the Landers' family garage, which was only good enough to house squirrels. It was dilapidated enough to fall apart at any given moment, the same garage where I found the BB Gun. The garage was easy enough to get into because the back door had fallen off..No I didn't...It was so wide open that a fat man could make it through, like the size of Jackie Gleason. I'm surprised the town didn't condemn it.

Night started to fall and on this night I was really bored, so I decided to mosey into the garage to see what kind of junk was in there. Let me make one thing perfectly clear, I did NOT intend to steal anything, I never did that, I was only curious. I didn't have a flashlight, but I just happened to have a book *of matches. Bet you guessed it--I lit a couple to see what was in there. They didn't seem to light very well, so I kept tossing them in a fiber drum. I finally quit then went home. I was in the kitchen when my aunt came in yelling "George move your car, the garage is on fire!" We all ran out to see the fire. My dad was able to get the car out without any damage. Within minutes the fire department came to put out the blaze.*

I stood in back of the crowd shaking like a leaf, trying hard to not look guilty. I was sick with fright. I could see me in handcuffs carrying a ball and chain wearing striped pajamas and having bread and water three times a day. If anyone would have asked me right away if i knew anything I would have soiled my self.

The next morning as I passed the garage on my way to the store, I could see many roasted squirrel carcasses burnt to a crisp. On the way back I cut through the Landers' yard and their daughter asked me if I saw anyone in their garage. I looked at her and quietly said,"No." She said that the fire chief said the fire started in a fiber drum. There were many roasted squirrels that day--could have been my ass.

CHAPTER SIX

BACK TO SCHOOL

CHAPTER SIX

BACK TO SCHOOL: Oh Crap

As I progressed through school, the years got tougher. My second grade year was no exception. My psycho nun this time was Sister Amobilia {automobile for short}. You're probably wondering just how awful could second grade be; it's a time for learning. Well, I'll tell you this much, it started the path to learning to hate mean people. Catholic School at St. Simeon was like biting shoe leather and having the shoe win.

My classmate next to me was the lovely Karen Boge { pronounced bowg-eee }. I had a crush on her, big time. Once, I went to the store to buy two packs of baseball cards at a nickel a pack. I came across this pretty necklace that cost a dime. I thought I could buy it and give it to her the next day, the only problem was, I only had a dime and the new set of cards just came out. I had to think fast about this. I took the necklace off the rack, went down middle the isle, stuffed it in my pants, grabbed the two packs of cards and paid for those, then walked out. I might add that, in those days, there was no sales tax for purchases under a quarter, so I paid with even change.

The next day, I gave her the necklace. When I gave it to her she had a big smile on her face, a smile that could lit up a darkened sky. She was very happy. I put it on her and she gave me a peck on the cheek {face}. Ooh! My first kind of kiss. Enough mush, she got the necklace, I got a kiss and the baseball cards.

This one incident happened when I came to school not feeling very well. I felt like I had a little bug running around in my stomach and literally causing me to run to the bathroom--"The runs" we called it. Having tension of just going through another day of school wasn't helping matters.

All things considered I guess I had to pay for my past sins. When class started I felt more and more that I really, really had to go to the bathroom again. Sister Amobilia didn't like being interrupted while she was teaching. I raised my hand and she asked me what I wanted. I told her that "I'm feeling sick and have to go to the bathroom now." She snapped back and said, "Wait until recess." She got angrier as I persisted. She angrily told me to "Sit down and shut up." As I started crying, I just started to fill my pants. It was not only embarrassing, but also frightening. She grabbed my arm and told me to go home. Mean? Totally. If I had a gun she'd have been shot. My Grandma Altenhoff lived four houses down from the school so I ran to her house, she cleaned me up, called my mom to bring me fresh clothes. The hate for nuns was growing greater now.

There were several instances where I was caught throwing erasers at someone and was scolded across the hands with a wooden pointer that the nuns would use to point at things written on the chalk board. Yanking a girl's hair for fun was another reason to get whacked over the fingers.

This one time though, I was on "patrol" duty during lunchtime with my partner Scotty Bouloin {pronounced-balloon}. Our job as patrol boys was to let people cross the street safely. We'd have our patrol belts on. When someone wanted to cross the street {always corner to corner, no jaywalking} we would go to the middle of the street and extend our arms out from the side- this meant that all cars must stop and wait until the person was safely across. We then would put our arms down and walk off the street.

On this afternoon Scotty and I were bored so we tossed around a small dodgeball, slightly smaller than a beach ball, but more the size and weight of a volley ball { I would have said that before but I couldn't think of it till now}. Anyway, Scotty threw it to me and I missed it, and the ball went into the mud puddle. Scotty bent over to pick up his pencil then I quickly picked up the muddy ball and threw it at him and hit him between his butt cheeks. He had mud all over his shiny new pants. Not a good match since his pants were brown and the mud was black. I couldn't stop laughing - it was so funny.

Scotty didn't think that it was so funny. He reported it to the head of the patrol boys, who just happened to be my brother. I still couldn't stop laughing - just looking at those pants. As long as my brother was the head of patrol boys I didn't have to worry much, so I thought.

When lunchtime was over we all filed back two by two to the classroom. When we all sat down and settled in my brother came in still wearing his patrol belt then began talking to my teacher, Sister DeLurd. After my brother left, Sister DeLurd did not look too pleased.

She called my name and told me to stand up. She told me to hand over my patrol belt, clear the books out of my desk and to go home and not come back without my mother or father. I did that without argument.

I was really pissed off now. I couldn't wait for my brother to get home. I was waiting. I didn't care if he was two years older than me, he was going to get his.

When my brother got home he was razzing me about the incident and he thought he was pretty funny. You don't razz me when I'm already riled. For me, being tossed out of being a patrol boy, after wanting to be like him, and also being thrown out of school because of him, then laughing at me, this was the last straw--I hauled off and gave him a swift punch to the side of his face, throwing him off balance and falling to the floor.

I didn't stop there. I was so full of fight I kept on hitting him.
   In the heat of the fight I grabbed his pencil out of his top pocket and stabbed him in the left arm, and broke the lead off, my sister was a witness. My mother finally pulled me off and separated us. There were ill feelings between us for a very long time, I no longer wanted to be like him, I was officially me, my own way from now on, whether anyone liked it or not.

BE CAREFUL OF THE STONES YOU THROW:
  Honesty Is Not The Best Policy

   This story takes place in the seventh grade, Sister Alberta presiding. Construction was now underway on the new convent-the nuns new home which is located directly across the street from my school. We called it "The nun's nut house." Dave Ariola and I grew to be pretty good friends, a couple of good mischief-makers. We always hung out in the morning recess and at lunchtime. This day was a very memorable one for both of us. Dave and I were feeling a little antsy for some action. We were standing in the stone covered lot, where the new church stands today. We were talking, picking up stones to throw and pass time. We noticed the bricklayers on the scaffold weren't doing a whole lot so, as we started to stare and grin at each other, Dave came up with an idea to get them working again. We were going to have some fun. We each picked up a handful of stones, moved within shooting range and started to let 'em fly one at a time. I knew we hit at least two of them because one of them was holding his leg, the other was holding his arm. They started yelling vulgar words at us and calling us vulgar names.
   The bell sounded to end lunchtime. It was time to line up two by two and walk back to class. Sister Alberta was a little late coming back to class. Dave and I sat grinning at each other until Sister Alberta walked in all red faced. Dave and I were softly laughing; we thought that she was either mad or had been at the bottle. We thought that she looked pretty funny.
   She closed the door and demanded to know who the two boys were that were throwing stones at the workers. She demanded they stand up. Dave and I figured, "If we were honest, punishment would be minimal." So, at the same time we both stood up. She pointed to Dave first and told him to follow her to the boiler room. There's no doubt about what was going to come down. The boiler room was not used for private discussions. Sister left the doors open so we would hear Dave yelling in pain with each blow to his butt with the broom handle. I didn't count the whacks he was getting. I was still standing and everyone was looking at me, knowing what I was in for.

HONESTY----{con't}

I quickly stuffed my soft cover-spelling book in my pants to soften the blows. "She'll never know," I thought.

When Dave came back all red faced, he was made to stand in front of the class. Sister Alberta was a little smarter than I gave her credit for; she noticed the bulge in the back of my pants and made me discard it immediately. I had to oblige, unwillingly of course. I don't recall the number of whacks that I got but it felt never-ending. Crying for help did absolutely no good. I was also made to stand in front of the class the rest of the day. I think the punishment was made easier by standing up. I don't think we would have been able to sit.

So I leave you with this: "Be careful of the stones you throw, and honesty is not always the best policy--lying sometimes helps."

EAR TO EAR

Grade 5, Sister "Psycho" Edward presiding. She was the psycho of all psychos. She should have been a dominatrix. If she was married to God it couldn't have been too long because she was banished to St. Simeon School, for what? I know not.

After lunch the class was given two flash cards with one word on them and when called upon you had to make a sentence with each of them. Mine were "vessel" and "remarked" which I knew nothing about.

Scotty was next and the nightmare's begin. His first one was easy. The second word he was stumbling with.Sister Edward stood behind him and as he stumbled again she started slapping both ears repeatedly. He started crying profusely and she lost control and slapped his ears some more. After awhile she gave up and told him to sit down. She then called on me. As I made my way up there I was warned of the consequences. I knew for a fact I was going to get it too because I had no clue what "remarked" even meant. My first word went by without incident. I felt the pressure, I knew she was behind me--waiting. I told her that I didn't have a sentence for it. She said angrily, "Make one up." I said, "I didn't know." I was crying my eyes in front of everyone. I could see Scotty still crying. She slapped me a few more times still yelling at me. Slapping a couple more times, she gave up. My mother came by to pick me up and I told her what happened. She went in to see Sister Edward. I never knew what took place in there.

To this day I still feel hatred for her. I think if I ever saw her again I would come up behind her and slap her ears. I did hear some time later that she was committed to an institution. I deserved punishment for things, but this was too extreme. She should have been jailed.

41

ON THE LIGHTER SIDE: MY LIFE ON THE STAGE

Ahh! The stage, not the one cowboys use, but the one where persons can show off their talent. I use the word"Talent" very loosely here. Today it is called "Performing arts." The stage: A place where you can be someone else, like Shakespeare, John Wilkes Booth, Jack Benny, Dean Martin, or George Burns to name a few.. When your act is over you take your bows in front of adoring fans, with thundering applause, standing ovations, even an encore or two. It's moments like this that you feel that you're on top of the world, adored by everyone.

I needed a good intro here. I hope the build up was as exciting for you as it was for me to bring it to you. All actors need a little confidence to help their careers that may lead to fame and fortune.

Unfortunately, I was not writing about me, because I fell victim to, not lack of talent, but lousy roles and bad scripts. If you don't have good roles and well-written material, you lose before you start. See if you agree. Here are two examples.

Back in second grade I was in a musical called "I'm Forever Blowing Bubbles." Sound good so far? We rehearsed for a whole week. This will knock your socks off. The show was to start like this....Ready? There were six of us boys holding these huge multicolored lollipops. When the theme song started to play we were to parade to the other end of the stage in single file. Now picture this if you will. Here goes. When we started our march we would stop for a second, raise our right foot for a second, then step forward, stop, then raise our left foot. So it went right up, left up. After getting to the other side we would quickly go back stage and hide behind the cardboard cut-outs that looked like giant bubbles. You could notice that they weren't real because of the smeared color chalk marks. Anyway, as the curtain rose and the music continued, we were blowing our bubbles and the girls came out in these silly costumes and doing their silly dance and we were still blowing our silly bubbles. I ran out of bubbles before the show was over because I had a smaller bottle.

When I was told that I was gonna dance I thought it would be a "Soft Shoe" or a "Sand Dance." When everyone was doing right up, left up, I was at least noticed the most because I was doing the opposite--left up, right up. When the performance was over there wasn't any standing ovation or any requests for encores. My talent was quickly going to waste here. I needed better parts to show off my talents. Better writers, choreographers too. Better things are headed my way...gotta be.

I was now in third grade. I was asked to to another performance. My mind raced, thought process was now activated again. "Hollywood, here I come at last." Maybe a chance to meet Lassie too. How exciting. I was going to do a speaking role, not some silly walk-on part. This was "IT," the big time, my big chance. I thought for sure now, bright lights of Broadway maybe? My career was ready to take off.

This act consisted of Jody Phil {pronounced - peel} and Bobby Verpaele{ we called him "buckets}, and , of course, me. This act, as it would turn out, no one was gonna see my face because we had to wear masks, although I would stand out anyway because of my thick, coke bottle glasses. How could I be missed?

I don't think I mentioned what the act was! Actually , I was giving this a big build up. I know the tension is building here. We were playing the world famous "Three Little Kittens." We had rehearsed all week for this and the last rehearsal was with costumes, dress rehearsal. Our costumes fit us all pretty well except the tail was broken off and my mother had to sew it back on. My tail didn't curl like the others either, but it didn't matter much to me because I figured, "Who's going to look at my tail anyway? I was hoping no one would step on it and tear it off. We all knew our lines and were ready for the big show on Saturday night.

Saturday night, showtime was here, the hall was packed-my mother was in the front row with the neighbor lady. We were next. We took our positions on stage. Jody was on my left,Bobby on my right and I was in the middle. When the curtain rose I saw my mother in the front row. We started with "We"re three little kittens who lost their mittens," Jody then delivered his lines first, then me---I could see my mother in the front row. Jody whispered my lines to me and kept nudging me. Bobby then did my lines and his. Me? I could see my mother in the front row. Then the curtain came down. I couldn't see my mother in the front row.

Obviously my career was over, besides, whoever heard of talking kittens anyway? I was the true cat. My chance to meet Lassie was now only a fantasy. No Hollywood. To this day I still haven't met Lassie. As for my mother in the front row, she occupies the front row in heaven as of January 11, 1962. She'll always be "in the front row" of my heart.

MY LIFE ON THE STAGE

MY RETURN TO THE STAGE 2006

CHAPTER   SEVEN

THE

HOOD

{ MISADVENTURES]

THE HOOD: Misadventures

My father and I were never close, not even "buddies" of any kind because we never really did anything together as a father and his son. The best time I ever had with him was when he and my uncle took me to my first ever professional baseball game between the White Sox and the Boston Red Sox at Comiskey Park to see "The Splendid Splinter," Ted Williams play. To this day, I consider him the greatest hitter of all time. The Red Sox lost 3-0 and Ted went 0 for three at the plate.

I had only fear of my dad because when he got angry at something I did or didn't do he would use the belt on me and on some occasions, I got quite a whipping. I will say this though, he never laid a hand on me or used any kind of physical force. I felt a lot of leather, more than my brother or sister. There were times I actually hated him. I never got close to him even when I grew up and got married. I had so much resentment toward him that it got to the point that it was irritating just to be around him.

One late Saturday afternoon he and I took a walk to Tony's house next to the park across Washington Blvd. Tony would later move to the other side of town. My dad dropped me off at the park and told me to stay there until he came back to get me.

The park seemed big to me. It had a sandbox, teeter tauter, big and little slides, swings and monkey bars. This day I had the park all to myself, no one else. After about an hour I was getting quite bored. Figuring maybe my father forgot me, I went home.

When I arrived my mother asked me where my father was. I knew right away that he didn't forget me. I answered back,"He's at Tony's." A short time later I hear the door open and him yelling out, "Is Richie here?" With that I ran to my room and put the covers over my head like a tent thinking that he'll never find me..he did, the blankets flew off and I already started to cry. Within seconds the belt came off his waist and the swinging began. I began shouting, "No! No!" All I can remember was that evil look in his eyes and his face with teeth clenched taking swing after swing. This defintly was not "Little House On The Prairie.

FISHING TRIP

This story is about the only time we ever went fishing together. It was an overnighter at Green Lake, WI. We stayed with Tony's older brother, "Old Joe" as we all called him. He let us use his rowboat. This short trip was a disaster.

FISHING TRIP {con't }

We were fishing the opposite side of the lake away from "Old Joe's" cabin and caught a couple of striped bass. My dad had a big one the line and when he got it near the boat I grabbed the dip net to haul 'em in. I reached over the side of the boat to land the fish and my glasses fell off and into the water. My dad was furious. We hauled the fish in but from that time on all he did was piss and moan about how much the glasses cost him and what it would take to replace them. All I could remember him saying was, "Do you know hard I have to work to get new ones? God, Rich! " Of course I didn't know. I was just a seven -year old kid. We never fished together again.

WHERE'S "TOOTS"

My sister's name was Dianna who was three years younger than me. Her nickname was "Toots." Where that name came from, I know not. This is a classic story around our family circle that will last for as long as any still possesses this book.

We had a blue 1952 Plymouth; everybody else was driving Fords or Chevys. To us kids the car seemed enormous, very spacious and seat belts were not required at that time. The cars of that era were made os solid steel and was considered pretty safe. Often we'd go over to our cousins Norma and Art or go over to cousin Pat's house.

It was getting pretty late and it was time to head for home, so us kids would file in the car with me in the back on the driver's side, my brother in the middle and "Toots" behind my mother's side. Cozy? We were getting a little restless and giggling while my parents were talking. We were on Washington Boulevard heading toward home. Toots was playing with the door handle when the door suddenly came open and Toots fell out. Dad thought we opened the window and asked us to close it. My brother and I just looked at each other afraid we'd get hit if we said anything. My dad turned around and yelled out, "Where's Toots? I softly said, "She fell out." Dad was furious but more worried. He turned the car around and saw her sitting on the pavement. This all happened so fast. Fortunately the speed limit was only 30 mph. It seemed like a long time. MY dad called my Uncle Hank to come over and watch us while he and my mom took Toots to the Joslyn Clinic. I remember thinking, "What's he going to do to us," momentarily not thinking whether or not she's Ok. When they got home, Mom put her in the crib. I couldn't help laughing inside as to how funny she looked all scuffed up with scrapes and bruises. She was all right, Nothing serious. She lived a short but happy life. She died October 18, 2006 57 yrs. old.

   This story is short but a very true story that my sister and I
agreed that I should put this one in my book.   We laughed
about
it constantly every time we were together at family
get-togethers.   Only her and I knew about this one.   Everyone
tried to get us to tell but we never broke the silence.   The last
time
that I saw her alive she said to me, "Rich! You gotta put this in
your book."   Most of you who are reading this are probably
family so you automatically understand the family sense of
humor.   I think you might find the humor in this as well as
Diane and I did.   The family wait is finally over, so here it is.
   Diane and I were sitting on the kitchen floor playing.   She
then came up with an idea.   "Why don't we play house.?   You
be the father and I be the mother!" she said with a great big
smile.
Pretty logical so far. We had pretend kids.   Even more logical.
They were outside playing somewhere, being our kids, they
were probably playing in the street, where else?   Di {we called
her Di for short} and I went upstairs to play house up there
while everyone else was watching TV in the living room.   Di
was wearing this ugly green flannel night gown with little girls
on it.   I had this neat looking pair of PJ's with Roy Rogers and
his horse Trigger on them.   For no apparent reason we just
started laughing {we still do that}.   Then we pulled the blanket
over our heads as if we were in a tent.   The question the was,
"What do you want to do next.?"   Now   we couldn't
remember
which one of us asked the silly question and which one
answered it.   Well, we were still laughing so hard at the
question.   Ready folks?   The answer was, "Lets' smell asses!"
We were still laughing so hard we couldn't stop.   Then all of a
sudden the blankets flew off of us with hurricane force and all
at once our loud laughter turned into ice cold fear, fear like
we've never known before.   Our father went ballistic.   He
yelled at me so loud   to "go down stairs" that it was deafening.
He threw me off the bed and reached for his belt.   I quickly ran
down stairs and sat in the chair on the porch.   All I could hear
was the belt making contact and my sister screaming her head

off and yelling to Toots, "I'll show you.. smelling asses?" I was next. I was ready to soil myself. I could hear his rushing footsteps, coming after me. He pulled me off the chair and raised his belt high in the air for a real good swing. I could have waited longer but my father insisted that it was going to be NOW. He showed no signs of weakness. To this day I can still see the fire in his eyes. All the crying and screaming I did didn't change his mind. I don't know how many whacks I got, it felt never ending, but our asses knew for sure.

To this day we still don't know who started it or where the term came from. Spur of the moment? Don't know..I assure you that we never played house again.

DIANNA AND ME: BEING CREATIVE

My sister and I got along pretty well not much arguing etc.,
nothing earth shattering. We were creative in our own way.
When we were together we always found something to do.
Playing house again was not one of them.

There was a kids show on TV called "Elmer The Elephant,"
hosted by John Conrad. The show featured a fake elephant
head with someone's hand and arm in the trunk. Elmer
couldn't talk, so John would ask Elmer, yes or no questions
and Elmer would nod his head up and down for "yes" and
move his head sideways for "no." A lot of times Elmer would
use his trunk to knock off John's head, I mean knock the hat
off John's head..no violence on kid shows.

Diane and I decided to create our own version of the show.
We had a window in our kitchen and on the other side was
our enclosed porch. I would be on the porch side, put my
sister's coat over my head, stick my arm in the sleeve and thus
I became Elmer. She would sit on the kitchen side and sit on
the chair next to the window and she would be John Conrad
wearing one of my hats, and on occasion I would knock the
hat off of her head. If that didn't sound exciting catch this
next episode of being creative.

Another show that we poorly copied or tried to copy was the
Saturday night "Dick Clark Show." It was a spin-off of
Clark's weekly "American Bandstand." The Saturday show
would feature artists that would perform their latest hits.

The way our show worked was that each of us would take
turns being Dick Clark then the other would perform
someone's hit record by playing the record then we would lip
sync to the song. I liked Duane Eddy, guitarist, inventor of
the "Twang." Now here's where being creative comes in, this
might amuse you..Since we didn't have a guitar and no talent
to go with it, I simply used a wooden handle from my bamboo
pole and would imitate Duane Playing that twangy guitar.
My sister would put the record on and I would strum the
stick. How about that? I sounded just like him
too...MMMMM. When it came to singing we sometimes would
be male or female, didn't matter to us, we did both.
Fortunately for us while we were doing all this the rest of the
family was outside in the yard or being elsewhere. If that's
not being creative, you tell me..what is?

MUD BALLS

After a pretty rainy morning my friend Johnny came by
calling for me to come out. In those days we would knock first
then call out the person's name this way: Oh John ney,"
pause "Ooh John ney." One day I went over to Johnny's
house and called out for him. His mother Flo came out and
said, "You know Johnny has no arms or legs." I said, "I
know, we just wanted to use him for third base."

MUD BALLS {con't}

That really didn't happen, I thought we needed a little humor so I thought to throw that in. Maybe I should throw it out.

Getting back to this much-anticipated event, Johnny came out and we hung out for awhile. His parents came out and said they were going out for a little bit. They told us to stay out of trouble. We went out side and sat by the curb. We grabbed a couple sticks and started to poke holes in the mud. That doesn't sound like much fun or anything too exciting, but we couldn't find anything else to do. We weren't exactly loaded with ideas. All of a sudden it hit us. Why not make some mud balls? We'll throw them at street lights. Is this getting exciting yet? Wait! There's more. One shot got away and hit the white portion of Johnny's house. The "splat" was funny sounding. Sounded like a suction cup being pulled off of something. We both burst out laughing. This was more fun and easier than trying to hit street lights.

So we pelted the house for a little while. When we ran out of ammo his house looked like it had black polka-dots. When his parents got home, John Sr. was fit to be tied. He was definitely not a happy man. He called my father to "Take a look at what your son did to my house." My father was hotter than a firecracker, but he also knew that I didn't do it alone. We both apologized to John and I was the only one who had to wash it off. No belt this time.

ONE HORSE TOWN

Overall Bellwood was a pretty quiet town except around 24 th St. There was always some kind of "Action" around as previous stories have related. "Nothing ever happens around here until Rich learned how to walk." That quote was from the four-eyed snitch next door {BB gun story?}.

Sometimes boredom would take over and I would go in the alley and throw stones and use old man Rymshaw's fence as a target. He never liked me, he said he was tired of picking up stones in his yard. Well! There was nothing else to aim at, what do you expect a boy to do? Today, you kids reading this are very spoiled compared to my generation. Being creative, remember?

The term "One Horse Town" really fit this part of the hood because once a week an old man would ride his horse and wagon down our alley from Madison St. to the south of us to St. Charles Rd. to our north; about four blocks. He'd tap two pieces of iron together and call out, "Rags and old iron, rags and old iron." If you had any of these he would stop and collect them from you. He always wore the same clothes which consisted of a ragged black hat, ragged coat, and pants. He looked like a real life dirty old bum, must have been poor. Sometimes he would stop by our yard and put the feed bag on. {The horse not him}. The bag was full of oats and I watched him eat for awhile, and I'd get to pet him. {the horse, not the man}.

It would be pretty silly to think that the old man would actually put the feed bag on his own face, wouldn't it? and then let me pet him instead of the horse? While all this was going on the old man would chat with Mom.

One day the old man came by and didn't stop. I told the crabby old buzzard to wait. He told me to get out of the way. He must not have realized just who he was talking to. "I'll show him," I thought to myself. So I did what any red-blooded kid from "The Hood would do, I picked up a stone and threw it at the horse. I was lucky enough to graze his ass, the horse's ass not the old man's. The old horse reared up and went "HEEEE! or whatever old horses do when hit in the ass with a stone. The horse started to go a little faster and the old man yelled back, "I'll tell your mother you little bastard." "Tell her!" I yelled back. Without much energy, the old man stopped the nag before getting to the street.

Weeks went by and no sign of the old manor his horse. Guess I showed him. I asked my father why the old man wasn't coming around anymore and dad said, "He died." It was the end of an era of the horse, the wagon and a ragged old man saying, "Rags and old iron, rags and old iron." That would never be heard again. The glue I was using must have been made from his hide,{ the horse's, not the man's } I couldn't get the glue to stick to anything. Payback? Maybe. What goes around comes around.

WATERMELON CAPER

I wasn't your average kid in the hood. I was creative, crafty, shifty, and sneaky. Smart too. I knew how to press people's buttons without being a smart aleck or foul mouthed.

This adventure targets old man Rymshaw who lived on the other side of the alley next to the vacant lot on 23rd st. The lot was across from our yard. He had a pleasant wife, beautiful daughter Darlene.

Old man Rymshaw was always a cranky old shank who never smiled at any thing or anyone. He would use the vacant lot for his garden. His garden was a pretty good size. If he knew nothing else, he knew how to plant and take care of a garden. He'd plant radishes, carrots {yum, yum} tomatoes and watermelons {mmmmm}. I'd steal carrots one in awhile and was caught once and was threatened to be shot with his shotgun if he catches me again. His threats didn't scare me, his so called shotgun was only a BB gun. I should have stolen his. I had my mind set on one of those big watermelons this time, and by golly I was gonna get me one.

On one dark night{as they usually are}, I decided it was time to make my move. The watermelon was ripe and just the right size.

WATERMELON CAPER {con't}

The moon was in it's new stage, which means there wasn't any. Pitch black except for the streetlights. There happened to be one right in front of his garden but somehow it got broken earlier in the day, probably by some shifty character. I called this a well-planned 'Hit." I was never questioned about staying out late during the summer as long as I hung around our square block. No one ever told me, "Don't go across Rymshaw's garden."

In our part of town most people were in bed by 10-10:30 pm. I went into our yard and stood by the tree and planned my attack on the old man's garden. Lights were out, no moon, no stars. It was time to make my move. The watermelons were on the far end of the garden near the street light. I couldn't snatch it from there because that meant that I would have to be exposed on the sidewalk. Couldn't do that. So I had to go in from the alley side where there was no lights at all. I had to crawl in on my belly all the way to the far end. As I got closer I could almost smell those luscious melons, not Darlene's--I was too young anyway. I could almost hear the melons saying,"Take me! Take me." Not Darlene's--I was too young. I didn't have time to be fussy. Like a commando, I quickly grabbed one and at the same time I heard a popping sound and just as fast a spray of dirt hit my face. The old man must have eyes in back of his head or he stays up 24 hours a day. I felt the next pop. A BB hit my butt and stung me. Lucky for me I had jeans on and the BB didn't penetrate. But I got that melon, boy! It was bigger than a stump. I ran north down 23 rd. St. so he would think that it was someone else. I had to wait awhile to come home because Rymshaw could see our door from his window. After about a half hour or so later I snuck into the house. Low and behold, guess who was up waiting for me--Mom. When she saw what I had she just smiled, patted me on the head and softly said, "Go to bed now, OK?" That was my MOM. I miss these little things about her.

BAD HUMOR MAN

I scream, you scream, we all scream for ice cream. What an intro for this next episode; creative,eh? Most of us enjoy ice cream at some point of our lives. Maybe you got yours from the "Good Humor Man" who drove the white truck with the big ice cream bar on the side. I was no different. It seemed to taste better right off the truck. The Good Humor Man wore a white uniform with a white policeman's type hat. He would pull a string that hung from the top of his windshield frame and that would result in having bells ring to let people know that he was coming.

BAD HUMOR MAN {con't}

The guy that came by our part of the hood was a very crabby person. His face was as red as a tomato and probably could pass for an American Indian Chief. He was very rude, never smiled. He seemed to like his job as well as someone would a nail up their keester. Instead of saying,"What could I get for you?" He would say, "Whatta you want?" He wasn't Italian, he just talked that way in a very cranky voice. You know what I say? "If you don't like your job or kids, then quit, don't come around,especially on 24th st. At least the ice cream man on the bike had more courtesy and manners.

My friends J.B. Milano and Johnny Huschik and I got to talking one day and devised a plan to give that old guy the old "what for," a taste of hell from the boys of the hood. maybe he would change his attitude a little or, we'd be the 24th st. unwelcome wagon.

We heard him coming again about a week later. He was headed south on 23rd st. toward Warren Ave. then down south 24th st. toward us. We each grabbed a couple of stones from the alley and hid behind separate bushes. A three-way attack was now in place. When he got within range we let our stones fly hitting the truck. We ran in separate directions and met each other at the Bell-May food and candy store on 22nd st. Worked like a charm, he couldn't finger any of us. Lesson here: Don't ever mess with the boys from the 24th st. side of the hood.

BOYS OF THE HOOD: THE DEMONS

This probably should have been put in the beginning of this chapter but I forgot. So it is now appropriate here because we are each two years older and don't feel like starting over.

The Demons, as we are called now, are all from 24th st. living within two or three houses of each other. We weren't called the Demons until after the bad humor man incident. A girl from 23rd st. by the name of Janet actually gave me the nickname, "Demon." I had a real crush on her and she knew it. I'd do little things to get her attention. That's another story, no space here for it. Anyway I chose the name , "The Demons" to honor her.

Anyway we were not a trouble making type gang, we could be if the need arises. We just hung out at night around the streetlights, jus BS-ing and throwing stones at the streetlights bulb to see who could break it first. We had dark blue wool jackets with a red stripe down each arm between thin white stripes. I was the leader followed by J.B., Johnny, and Norman. A good team that got along well together.

THE HANGING TREE; A CAT TAIL

One early evening we were hanging out on the corner when J.B. spotted this light brown kitten walking around our turf. Actually it was walking across the street, but saying, "Turf" sounded a little more tuff and dramatic. The kitten looked somewhat lost so we decided to help it out. We didn't see the mother at all, in fact, we never seen any cats in our part of the hood. We figured it might be kind of hungry so I went home and got a bowl, and since Johnny lived the closest to this area, he furnished the milk. It just so happened that we didn't have any cat food lying around.

After waiting a short time, this ignorant cat didn't want to eat, wasting good milk. I want to point out before I continue, if there are any animal activists out there, the statute of limitations on this ran out decades ago. Norman wasn't with us that day, so the three of us figured out what to do about this. We all would take care of the cat--our way. It made made no sense to let this cat live alone and turn out eating mice, etc. That would be cruel.

I just happened to have a four-foot long piece of rope in my pocket. I then made a make-shift hangman's noose on one end and put it around the cat's neck for a type of leash. We took him for a long walk to the other side of the big field which ran parallel to the rail road tracks. There was a tree near by about ten feet of the tracks. We all agreed as to what should be done next. Johnny held up the cat as I tightened up the noose. J.B. tied the other end of the rope to the tree branch. When we were set Johnny lifted the cat higher. On the count of three Johnny would drop the cat and hopefully the neck would break and the cat would die instantly. Unfortunately, it didn't work that way. The cat was squirming profusely. We let him squirm because we were afraid of getting scratched and possibly getting rabies.

After about an hour the clutsey cat refused to die, but was losing strength. We were dumbfounded as what to do next. JB came up with a brilliant idea. "Hold it! I have some firecrackers in my pocket." Well!! I just happened to have some matches in my pocket. So JB and Johnny put a firecracker in each of the cat's ears and one in it's mouth, then I lit all three. It hardly fazed the cat, but his stamina was almost nil. Our firecrackers weren't powerful enough. We all decided to go home and come back tomorrow.

The next morning we gathered together and moseyed to the field and check on the cat. When we arrived we could see from a distance that the cat was motionless. Presumed dead, we made our way to the "Hanging Tree" to make sure. When we got there the cat was stiff as a board.

HANGING TREE {con't}

Rigamortis had set in pretty well. The firecrackers had blackened his ears and mouth. He was a goner all right. We tapped him with stick to make sure again, and all we got was a "thud."

Cats are supposed to have nine lives. This one used 'em up all at once. We left him there and never returned. The Demons only lasted one more year by our own agreement. We never did anything like that again since. I was the very last one to leave"The Hood."

WERE YOU SMOKIN'?

I had a friend across the street by the name of Dave Carlson. He was as tall as an oak tree compared to my size. He was muscular build and a couple of years older than I and, like me, he didn't have many friends.

Once in awhile, a few of us would hang out with him in his back yard, mostly at night. We'd sit by a campfire roasting green apples. One night he taught us how to smoke inhalation cigarettes. You start out taking dried leaves and rolling them in small portions of newspapers, light away and enjoy. Really didn't taste very well, though it was a peaceful way of getting summer kicks.

Somehow my Dad found out but didn't say anything. He called me into the yard and sat me on the bench. I didn't know what was going on. I was brain dead--I couldn't think of anything that I could have done wrong--this time. He came back outside, lit a cigarette, one of his "Lung Burners" as he called them. They were a pack of "Lucky Strikes." The commercial said "L-S-M-F-T, Lucky Strikes means fine tobacco." Our version was "L-S-M-F-T" means loose straps means floppy tits. Consider the source and just go with it.

Waiting for something to happen, I just sat there, he didn't seem mad or anything. "I heard there was smoking last night by the Carlson's, were you smokin'? Before I could say anything he said,"Don't worry son, it's OK! I see you're ready to be a man now." He paused a moment, I was sitting still, I wasn't ready to poop, yet. "If you're gonna smoke, smoke like a man, don't use newspapers, it's not good for you." He lit one up and gave it to me. He showed me the right way to inhale and exhale. It was putrid. About half way done i felt sick, I had to throw up. I did make it to the toilet and it seemed forever to get done. Headaches followed for hours. I went back out and he offered me another one, smiling as he did so. I declined--forever, never tried again, but at age fourteen, I took up a pipe briefly.

56

VACATION-1953

Every summer my family, along with My Aunt Eve and Uncle Junior, their daughters, Dorothy and Bernice{ my cousins},
would all pitch in and rent this huge cottage at Twin Lakes,
Wisconsin for a couple of weeks during the summer. Sleeping
arrangements were a little tight, but not really too bad.
Dorothy, Bernice and I would sleep in the same bed in the
tower next to the window, the window with the hornets in it.
It was hot this August trip and we were especially hot at night
because we couldn't open the window without letting the
hornets come in and share our room. The adult couples slept
in separate rooms. Back upstairs in our room, it was hard to
fall asleep because of all the buzzing going on. It got kind of
scary. My cousin Dorothy told me to pray and I would fall
asleep and in the morning everything would be OK. I did, it
was.

Morning could not come soon enough for us. From our
room, we could smell flapjacks and could hear Pop begging
for more. The adults always ate first but there was always
enough for everyone. The women would share the kitchen
duties and did it without any misgivings. We couldn't wait to
taste those flapjacks with Log Cabin Syrup.

After breakfast we went outside to wait out our half hour
before going into the water to swim for fear of getting the
cramps. The weather was warm and humid. I took a walk on
the pier to look at my favorite boat, the "Miss Christine." The
owner of the boat was never seen by any of us, so I never got
to see what lay under that tan cover.

When it was time to swim, we would all grab our towels
and inner tubes. In single file we'd step in the water and head
for the beach. I was always last in line. The beach was about
fifty yards from our cottage. After a couple of minutes I felt a
sharp pain in my foot. I looked down and saw the water
turning red with my blood. I immediately started screaming
for help. Suddenly, a man from "Ackerman's Tavern" came
running out, picked me up, and wrapped my my towel around
my foot. The man carried me to the fence and handed me
over to my Dad. At the same time I saw my inner tube floating
away. I then started screaming out, "My inner tube, my inner
tube! Somebody get my inner tube!"

It took the doctor some time to stitch me up. I didn't cry all
the while. He said I was a good patient and as a reward he
gave me a plastic toy tugboat. On the way back we heard
something hit the car, then again. It was hailing. My Dad
parked the car as close to the cottage as possible. As I was
being carried in, a piece of hail rolled off the roof and hit me
in the noggin. I had to finish the vacation sleeping on the
screened in porch. The next year we found out that Jake, the
owner, had died and his wife sold the place. We never
returned

BOOGERS ON THE WALL

Have you ever heard of boogers on the wall? No? Well, you're about to, so sit tight. In the beginning of this book you may remember that my brother and I had to sleep together because of our small house. There was hardly enough room for the two of us because I had three Teddy Bears as well. Had to take care of them too.

My brother's nickname was "Butch." Don't know where that came from. Well, every once in awhile we would switch sides of the bed. In the summer I would sleep on the right side, because neither of us had to get up. In the fall I would sleep by the window because Butch had to go to school. Not promising anything but, this could get exciting for you. You feel the suspense yet? Once in a while I would have a nose full of boogers and my thinking was that it would be rude and inconsiderate of me to climb over him just to blow my nose, right? So I did what any normal five-year old kid would do; I planted them along the wall just below the height of the mattress. If you think about it--it makes more sense than putting them on the pillow or blankets, because they'd wind up in your hair or on you face. True? Sooo! where else could they go? Because of my small arms I had to do a little each time. Eventually it became somewhat noticeable because that part of the wall was a little darker than the rest of the paint job.

One Spring Saturday morning my mother decided that it was time for Spring cleaning our room. My brother and I helped move the bed so she could clean the floor and the walls..."Walls! Oh No! Not the walls! Oh My! From where she was standing she could see the different color of a certain part of a certain wall. I was standing in front of the spot hoping that she wouldn't see it. She kept asking me to "move over." I pretended to be trapped between the wall and the bed. Mom managed to get closer and was either shocked at what she saw or was confused as to what was going on. She took a closer look and asked me "What is this on the wall?" Without hesitation I blurted out; "Butch did it." My mother knew better. She took a closer look and was flabbergasted. She called my father over to show him the messy wall. It wasn't easy to explain. No belt. We did have to clean it up. Funny thing though, it was so dried up that we had to scrape it off first,then wash the walls and the floor. The walls had to be perfect because my dad had to repaint them and he definitely did NOT want us to do painting. Dad said,"If I find any more of your boogers on the wall I'll cut off your noses." To this day I use Kleenex or paper towels....My walls are always clean.

THE HOODS' LANDMARKS
(WHAT'S LEFT)

BELLWOOD FOOD SHOP

FINKS' CANDY STORE

CHAPTER   EIGHT

AGE OF DISCOVERY:

GIRLS

AGE OF DISCOVERY: GIRLS

I always knew there were girls on the planet and even in my neighborhood, but couldn't understand why or what made them so different from us boys other than being giddy with funny looking hair and wearing silly dresses.

My first encounter with one came when I was 5 or 6 right in my own home. I was playing with my toy truck on the porch floor and my mother put my sister on the toilet so Diane could go pee. Well needless to say, when I pushed my truck it went into the bathroom and went under our four-legged tub. I went to retrieve it and in doing so, I saw my sister going pee. I stared a moment and didn't quite understand why she didn't have anything down there like I have. I shrugged it off thinking that it probably takes a long time to grow one.

As the years progressed in grade school I discovered that the girls seemed to be getting prettier. Their hair appeared to be longer, and from the magazines I saw I knew that nothing was going to grow between their legs. The magazines was in reference to a previous story about the fire in the trench.

We had some girl grow really beautiful during my last three years of grade school like, Kathy Shilka, Camille Romano, Patty Chapeske, Celeste Allinson, Susan Peck and Susan Diverde. Many more, but the one that really stands out the most was a long-haired, blue-eyed blonde by the name of Jeannie Klouda. To me, she was every bit of perfection. She had a smile that would make you melt right on the spot. She was definitely created for all mankind to love her forever. I was lucky enough to see her again about 9 years later at one of my hockey games. I was coming out of the locker room headed for the ice when I saw her. As gorgeous as ever, long blonde hair and everything. We said hello and talked only for a few minutes. It turned out her husband was the opposing goaltender. He was also on the Bellwood police force. I never saw her again.

In our seventh grade class Sister Alberta decided to change our seating arrangements. As luck would have it, Jeannie sat right in front of me and Eddie Hahn was seated next to me. Eddie was as mischievous as I was. Our desks had tops that you had to raise to get anything out of it and the front of the desk had an ink well. For us they were empty because we were now using cartridge pens.

On several occasions, just for fun, I would put water in my ink well, take the cover off and dunk the end of Jeannie's pony-tail in it. She would always turn around, smile and give me a wink.

Eddie and I hit it off right away, two of a kind. One day Eddie came up with a challenge for me. A quarter was at stake here.

The bet was that i couldn't dunk Jeannie's hair while Sister Alberta was in the room. For me, it wasn't much of a challenge because everyone knew that her and I liked each other, so it really didn't matter too much what I did as long as I didn't hurt her. We put our quarters out and waited for Jeannie to come in and sit down.What I didn't know was that Eddie had put real ink in the ink well and had already taken the cover off. It was just enough so that I wouldn't notice. Jeannie sat down, got comfortable, fluffed her pony-tail as always and sat back as far as she could. Sister Alberta was already at her desk. The stage was set. Jeannie put her head back anticipating that something was going to happen. Eddie and I looked at each other and nodded as if to say, "Now." I hit my target but inadvertently tugged too hard causing Jeannie to turn her head and her hair came out of the ink well. She was as shocked as I was. I saw about a half inch of blu-blond hair, Sister Alberta saw it as well. Sister Alberta took Jeannie to the washroom to get the ink out. I took both quarters.

When Jeannie came back she gave Eddie an evil look knowing fully well that it was his idea. Before she sat down she looked at me and gave me a smile and that wink. Sister Alberta wasn't so cordial. She took me into the boiler room and turned my butt black and blue.

A CRUSH SHE NEVER KNEW

Another short story but a fond memory that no one ever knew..till now. To describe Carol now would be most difficult because I haven't seen her for over fifty years since the one whole day at the beach and one whole day at our house in Bellwood. For me, if I was four years older it may have been my first summer love.

My family and I took a ride out to Griswold Lake in McHenry County, IL. We went to visit my Aunt Mary,and Uncle John and my cousin Pat. Us kids enjoyed swimming and playing on the raft. More fun arrived, Cousins Art and Norma came with their parents, my Uncle Hank and my Aunt Esther. They live around the other side of the lake.

This outing was especially fun because all of us kids were headed for the raft. Cousin Pat invited her friend Carol over to meet everyone and join in. I was amazed how beautiful she was. I was still in grade school then and the male hormones hadn't kicked in yet, but I knew I was excited to see her.

We all gathered atop of the raft and would play "King or queen of the raft." The idea was to push everyone off and be the last one standing.

Only one time was I king, this was it. Carol and I were the last ones on. It was going to be me or her. We were trying to get hold of one another for leverage. I remember this part well. We were near the corner of the raft, our hands were raised and clenched to each other's. Wheels were spinning in my head thinking of my next move. Hormones were starting to kick in, I think. I released my right hand from her left hand and I grabbed her by he waist and with one quick motion, pulled her close and both of us went off the raft. That was a thrill for me back then. That was the closest I had ever been to a girl in grade school. If I saw her today she probably wouldn't remember that or me.

Later that summer cousin Pat and Carol came out to Bellwood to spend time with my sister Diane. I was kind of excited that Carol was coming also. I was still in bed when they arrived. I was very much the shy type. I was still in my PJ's. I peeked through the key hole to see Carol sitting on the couch. Being shy and not knowing what to deal with girls, I got dressed and climbed out my bedroom window. I went through Old Man Nash's yard, out to the front of the house, then came back through the door and made off like I just got home. I was kind of afraid to see Carol because I didn't know what to do. I just knew that I had a crush on her and wished that I was older.

The girls walked over to the "Blue Bell" restaurant for lunch. I was hanging out across the street from there with a couple of the guys. When the girls came out and saw us they waved "hello." I said "Hi" to Carol and she said, "Hi" back to me. Pat and Carol were picked up later that day and have not seen her again since that summer day. No one ever knew that I liked her or had a crush on her. It was a summer fling that never was.

CHAPTER NINE

DEMOLITION MAN

Everyone in the family knows tis story except you grandkids. My close friends know about it and some of them never let me forget it-not that I could anyway. So for the last time, here it is.

Back in April 1963 the Montreal Canadiens hockey franchise {owned by the Molson Brewery Family} made an infamous trade that made their #1 fan, me, very angry. They traded hockey's greatest goaltender {at the time} Jacques Plante to the New York Rangers...For the ugliest and fattest goalie in the league, Lorne "Gump" Worsley. The name even makes me cringe.

In high school one of my subjects was printing class. I made some personalized envelopes and stationery for my class project.

When I heard of this trade I went ballistic. I told my Dad that I was going to write them and let them know just how I felt. My Dad just figured that I was just blowing off steam and ignored it. I went into my room and started writing. I called these people every conceivable name there was. I also told them these exact words, "If you don't get Jacques Plante back by August 1, I will blow up the Montreal Forum." I figured that would do it.

Later on, through an advertisement on TV, I sent for a brochure about buying land in Toltec, Arizona for $1995.00 per acre. It was quite appealing to me even though I had no money or job.

A few months went by and I thought everything just blew over. My Dad came home from work and said that he and I were going to Arizona the last week of July and the first week of August. Sounded like fun, although we had to take Route 66 via Greyhound bus.

About two days before the trip was to commence, I happened to be on the porch playing some Duane Eddy records while my sister and cousin Pat were doing their thing. Two guys dressed in suits and ties came to the door and just as fast as they pulled out their ID's they announced that they were from the FBI "Federal Bureau of Investigation." I was too scared to even remember their names. "Are you Richard Altenhoff?" Of course I said, "Yes" The agent showed me an envelope with my return address, asked to come in. By now I was ready to piss in my pants. Shaking like a tree in a tornado, I told them to sit down. They asked me, "Who's in the house with you?" I told them. Then they asked, "Who lives here in this house besides you?" I told them. The other agent pulled out the familiar letter from the envelope and showed it to me. The letterhead had the name and address torn off, the envelope did not. I tore it off because I thought that most people just throw away the envelopes anyway.

65

This time someone didn't. One of the Agents handed me the letter and asked me to identify it. I did, I told them that it was my hand writing. The Agent then told me to read it out loud. I couldn't hold the letter very still and read it at the same time without stuttering. The Agent made me pause and explain some of the intense vocabulary that I used to identify the owners of the Canadiens. He also told me the reason they were here. It was because threatening to blow up a building in any country is a Federal offense punishable by a very lengthy prison sentence. I was ready to fill my pants with liquid poop.

"We will be back soon to arrest you upon further investigation and do not leave Bellwood for any reason until you hear from us..is that clear?" Shitting in my pants was the least of my worries now. How do I plan to explain this to my dad? When he comes home I'd be better off dead, if not I will be.

When they left I made a B-line to the toilet..I wasn't kidding. I had to go, and go I did. A few hours later my dad came home and we all had supper, for me it was a quiet one. My father asked me if I was OK and I said, "I'm good." If I was really good, I wouldn't be in this mess. I couldn't help thinking that I had to tell him sometime, like real soon, like after dinner soon. There was no way out except suicide. "How could we go to Arizona now? If I leave and they find me gone, I'll be hunted down until captured or shot dead." These thoughts kept running through my head. I had to come right out with it.

After dinner we sat in the living room and, as usual, my dad picked up The "Chicago Sun-Times" then asked me, "Is there something on your mind?" I first reminded him of the letter then I told him that I actually sent it. He put down the paper and I started to tell him everything. In between sentences his fury was evident. His teeth clenched, his eyes were bulging out and his face was redder than a red pepper. I felt I was on death's door. After a few moments he said that we're going to Arizona anyway. Bring out the handcuffs.

We left for Arizona anyway, August 1st was only two days away. The Greyhound bus took down route 66. The longest days of my life lay ahead. Constantly looking to see if we were being followed. waiting to be arrested at the next stop. Feeling guilty of a crime not yet committed is terrifying, being a fugitive of justice. If the Forum blows up on August 1st I'll be fried a chicken in a skillet or hung by the neck until dead.

We checked in the hotel and my dad specifically said, "Do not answer the door for anyone till I get back."

DEMOLITION MAN {con't}

Some vacation. A little while later came a knock on the door. Panic stricken, I figured that I should answer it, put my arms out and let the cuffs go on, I was toast. By now I was ready to go. I had had enough of this and couldn't take any more. I finally got the courage to open the door even though I was told not to. I opened the door and there standing before me was the cleaning lady bringing us some towels. " The cleaning lady"-I repeated in my brain. I was sweating bullets. My heart was beating so fast it almost jumped out of my chest, but was happy to see her.

August 1st went by without the Forum blowing up, but I was still not off the hook. The FBI still had not come to get me, but I still had to go home. They knew I was gone. When we got home we found my Uncle Hank sitting on the bench in our yard. We no sooner got into the yard when my Uncle Hank made mention that I had made someone from Arizona very angry. Uncle Hank said that the man was from Toltec, Arizona to see me about some land that I was interested in buying. When this man was told that I was only 16, he was furious and left. My Dad threw up his hands in disgust, held his head and yelled out, "What the hell did you do now?" Let me ask this myself, "How could anyone get into so much trouble in only two weeks?"

At the time I didn't realize, but the letter that I had sent went to the older Molson brother, the "Honorable" Hartland Molson who was a member of the Canadian Parliament. I told my father that I was going to write a letter of apology to the Molson family and the Montreal Canadiens. My father said just one thing to me. "I want to read it and I will mail it."

I did write the letter and he did mail it.

CHAPTER TEN

MY LIFE IN

BASEBALL

MY LIFE IN BASEBALL

   For quite a few years Baseball was a big and important part
of my life, on and off the field. Like most boys, I collected
bubble gum cards. I remember walking home from Fink's
Candy Store with my new pack. I took the alley way because
it was shorter. I was looking at them all the while that I was
walking. As I approaching Washington Blvd. I was looking at
the "Bubba Phillips" card and without paying attention, I
walked into the street between two cars that were waiting for
the light to change. I crossed between them and felt a thump
and I was suddenly spinning around and fell on the street.
Fortunately, the cars in the left lane were slowing down to
stop for the light. Next thing that I remember was seeing
Florence, our neighbor, was propping me up in a sitting
position with her arms around me. I was obviously dazed
and told her not to tell my parents " because they're gonna be
mad." Next thing I knew, my parents were there along with a
big maroon ambulance. My Mom rode with me to Joslyn
Clinic. Turns out I only had a few bruises. The man whose car
I walked into was more shaken than I was. He apologized
many times. My father told him that it wasn't his fault and
wasn't going to press any charges. The police let him go
home. About a week later the guy brought over and gave me
my first ever, brand new Rawlings first baseman's glove.

MY TURN AT BAT

   I started playing little league at age 9, I think. I played in
Bellwood Minor League for the Cardinals. My baseball
heroes were Babe Ruth, Ted Williams and Ernie Banks.
I remember wanting to play shortstop like Ernie. I did
play that for a short time, then I was moved to third
base because the coach's son wanted shortstop. It was
pretty well established back then that I was good
enough to play any position with decent ability. I was
too young to be said that I was great, but the potential
was there. Very seldom was I ever seen without a bat
and glove around the hood. The older kids ignored me
until one day they were short one guy and asked me to
fill in. They stuck me in right field because no one ever
hits over there and they figured I wouldn't cause any
damage there. When they let me take my turn at bat
and saw just what I could do, everyone wanted me on
their team.

THE NATURAL

Coach Arthur Doll: "This kid has natural talent to be developed even more." I was quick to pick up on the fundamentals of the game, but for the life of me I could never turn double plays when I played shortstop or second base which is essential to play either of those positions. Even as I grew older and more developed , I still couldn't do it. No talent for those positions. No coordination. I could make plays and catch almost anything but. that was all. I never played those again.

We played a game at the park on 25 th Avenue and Madison St. and I actually hit a home run on the roof of Sleepeck Printing Co. I was as amazed as everyone else. As a minor leaguer, we had to play on grass. We didn't have a dirt infield until we got to the majors. We did not have uniforms. We wore our street clothes and a baseball cap. Everyone wanted to play in the majors just for the uniforms and a fence in the outfield, and dugouts along the baselines. Another game we had was played in the field across from my school and I actually hit a homer over the roof of the house outside the fence in left field. {see photos}. All of the coaches agreed that, "This kid can hit." I also stuck out quite a bit as well. When the season was finally over, the coach said, smiling, "Hope to see you next year."

MAJOR LEAGUES 1957

Making a team was never a "Gimme." We had to earn our way on by going to "try-outs." Nothing from last season meant anything. We were all old enough for the majors but we had to try-out. If you made it, you'd be called and told what team you were on. If you didn't make it you were told as well. It was already established that I could hit but, "What else could he do?" I eventually made Art Doll's Tigers team, but they had to position me. I started out at third base but eventually lost it to the assistant coach's son, Bernie Piagari. Sound familiar? I did some pitching, threw four no-hitters, but pitching wasn't for me. I needed to be where the action was. I wound up in the outfield. For sometime I couldn't get a grip out there. Then I was moved to play first base, which turned out to be my home position for many years. I wasn't too shabby there, I averaged only one error per year.

Hitting home runs was my trademark. Mr. Doll incorporated my speed by teaching me the art of stealing bases, especially home plate which I did five times that season, twice in one game. I made the second all-star team. The first all-stars were given to those who were going to move on to the next level. More established now, I was ready for the next season.

1958 LEAGUE CHAMPIONS

This was our year. Our second year of maturity really paid off. Excellent managing and coaching. As a team, we could do nothing wrong. We had it all together. I was hitting home runs and led the league again and was nicknamed, "The Stroker." Our defense and pitching was superb. Everyone excelled to the best of their ability. My first championship was, in deed, a memorable one. Four of us made the first all-star team as starters.

ALL-STAR TEAM: GREATEST THRILL

Making the first all-star team was a thrill for all of us. We dreamed of going to Williamsport, PA. for the Little League World Series in the single elimination tournament.

Our first game was in Hillside, Il. which is the next town south west of Bellwood. Behind Kenny Erdman's great pitching, we won 1-0. I went 0-3 with three strike-outs. The next game was against Maywood, which borders Bellwood from the east. I did not start this game.

We only played seven innings which was little league rules. Since we were the visiting team we batted first. and quickly took a 3-0 lead. By the end of six innings we were trailing 6-3 with only one inning left. We started it off with a base hit, man on first, one out. The Maywood pitcher walked the next guy to put runners on first and third. The next guy struck out. Now we had two on and two out. A home run would tie the game.

Maywood was now changing pitchers and the boys doing the scoreboard in centerfield were stomping their feet and chanting, "We want Altenhoff, we want Altenhoff." Then the fans behind our dugout began chanting as well. Mr. Doll came up to me and said, "Grab a bat. If Theobald gets on, you'll hit." I grabbed a bat and went to the on deck circle. The boys and the fans started chanting again. The Maywood pitcher looked at me with a half smile. I looked back at him and we nodded to each other as if we were saying, "Can't wait to face you." I had goosebumps from the noisy crowd. I also felt the respect between the Maywood pitcher and myself.

The first pitch to Eddie was a strike. The next pitch was low and outside for a ball. I couldn't help thinking, "Grand slam would put us in the lead." The next pitch Eddie swung and hit a ground ball to the second baseman. He threw out Eddie in one quick motion and the game was over. We were out. As is custom we had to shake hands with our opponents and wish them luck. When I was face to face with their pitcher, our handshake was a little harder. Feeling more respect for each other. He then said to me, Another time?" I answered back, "Yeah! Good luck." It was a bone chilling experience to feel that kind of respect from opponents.

Arthur Doll talked to us briefly after the game and simply told us. "You were the real champions out there because real champs show sportsmanship and I'm proud of all of you."

It was a great feeling what the fans did. It was very heart warming, being respected and appreciated by people, and by the opposition. I learned something that year, and it is this..It's not about the home runs you hit or how well or bad you play, but the sportsmanship you display on and off the field.

PONY LEAGUE 1960-1961-
408 ft.. BLAST

I was now ready for something bigger, the next level,The Pony League. Again try-outs, having to prove yourself all over again. I was confident that I would make it, and make it I did. In this level your team name was your sponsor's name. Mine was "Shipley's Green Store." I was lucky enough to wear #14 again-Ernie Banks' number. I was back at first base again.

One night we had a father-son game and my father actually played and got a base hit. Later in the game, Mr. Mazzone came up and got a base hit between me and "Buckets" Verpaele. Mr. Mazzone was a cocky kind of guy but in a fun way. He loved to show off and have fun. Joe Gange was our pitcher. I called for a time out and the umpire let me have it. I went to the mound and asked Joe to sneak me the ball which he did. When I got back to my position the umpire yelled out, "Play ball." Mr. Mazzone took few steps off the base, not knowing I had the ball in my glove. All in one motion I dashed over to Mr. Mazzone, tagged him with my glove, held up my hand and yelled out, "Got 'em." The umpire quickly called him, "Out." Mr. Mazzone kicked up some dirt {in fun} and put on a phony tirade. The fans loved every minute of it.He looked back at me, smiled, then said, "I'll get eve with you." I smiled back and softly said, "OK!"

I made the all star team again, but the year was not especially eventful. The next year I was playing for a new team..my sponsor was "Borg-Warner" and five years later I'd be employed there for the next 43 years.

Well this year, as always, I'd be playing against Carmen Mazzone's team. This one game in particular, Mr,. Mazzone decided to use left hander Pat Piper to pitch against us. In the game he had already struck me out twice and after each strike out he'd call over and say, "Hey Busher." which means minor leaguer. Mr. Mazzone kept on ragging me throughout. He always did it with class though.

PONY LEAGUE{con't}

The next time at bat, Piper was still having his way with us. We were down 3-2 in the last inning. We had two men on and only one out. As I grabbed my bat and making my way to the plate, Mr Mazzone leaned out of the dugout, waved his finger at me letting me know that he thought I was an easy out again. I just grinned at him. The first pitch was high and outside. Mazzone motioned to Piper to keep the ball lower. The next pitch was right in my wheelhouse. I swung and hit the ball hard to left-center field. The ball carried like it had wings. I was already touching second base when I saw it hit the Bellwood Pool on one short bounce. As I rounded third base I could see Mr. Mazzone with his hat in one hand and his other hand brushing back what little hair he had left. The pool was 410 feet from home plate and because of the real short bounce they told me the ball was hit 408 to 409 ft. When I got back to the dugout, I looked back at Mr. Mazzone. He smiled, tipped his cap and nodded. I did the same. We wound up winning 5-3. Mr Mazzone was a true sportsman.

MAZZONE'S REVENGE

We won the second half of the season without a problem. Now we were ready for the championship. We would be playing the winner of the first half, which just happened to be ...Mr. Mazzone's team. I still can't remember his team's sponsor.

Mr. Mazzone was wise enough to not pitch Pat Piper. He got burned once already. However it didn't really matter. We had one run on only three hits, they had five runs and six hits. I was held to three strike outs. Both teams played really well, errorless ball, good pitching and fielding. We lost the championship to a better team. That was simply Mr. Mazzone's revenge.

Mr. Mazzone was still coaching Pony League after I left to play in other leagues, More ballparks. I stopped at the field one night to watch a game and ran into Mr. Mazzone and the friend he was with. We shook hands with great respect for each other. He turned to his friend and said, "This guy was the best all around ballplayer that I have ever managed against." Quite a compliment coming from a classy guy. He respected all of us who played for or against him. I simply thanked him for giving me more knowledge of the game and the sportsmanship he showed to everyone.

I was lucky to see him one more time. As a matter of fact, we played on a coach's team together years later. I was assistant coach for my brother's team--The Pirates, in the American League. Carmen got a base hit, then I came to the plate. The first pitch was right down the middle of the plate.

I swung at it and it sailed far over the centerfield fence. Mazzone was waiting for me at the plate as he scored ahead of me. As I touched home plate to complete the home run, Mazzone was laughing. He gave me the high-five and he said to me, still laughing, "You'll never change, will ya? I simply said with a wide grin, "No!"

Turned out it was homer #337, my last homer. But more important than home runs was the relationships I formed over those years. Especially that of Carmen Mazzone. I never had the honor of playing for him. I found out a few years ago that he had passed away from a heart attack. His passing brought much sadness to me, but at the same time great happiness because of the fond memories I have of him that was the inspiration to relive in this book. I played with and against his son Rick many times and was enough to say that Carmen was a good father and grand father.

I thank God that he gave me the talent to play this great game for over thirty years. Lots of fun, heartaches, thrills, many friendships and memories.

I have one important memory here to relate. This was my final season. I was playing for Rubin's Sporting Goods at this time. We had a game in Cherry Valley near Rockford, Il. We had just finished our pre-game work out. I went to sit on the bench to relax for awhile. Our dugout was a chain link, not the usual type of dugout. After a few minutes, I felt someone poking me in the back. I turned around and there was this little boy, probably not more than seven. He held in his hand a small piece of paper and a pen. He looked at me and said, "Mister will you sign this for me?" I looked up and saw his mother, she smiled and nodded her head saying, "Yes." So I did and with a big smile the boy thanked me and told his mother what he just got. On my way home from the park I gave that some thought and it actually brought a tear to my eyes. The autograph meant a lot to that little boy and his mother. It brought back memories of my own mother sitting there. For once I felt very special in someone's eyes. Of all the sports memories I have, nothing compares to this one.

1958 LITTLE LEAGUE CHAMPIONS

1961 PONY LEAGUE CHAMPIONS

CHAPTER ELEVEN

THE DAY THE

MUSIC DIED

FEBRUARY 3, 1959

THE DAY THE MUSIC DIED

Music has been a part of my life since around age four. I know this because my brother, being two years older, started school before I did. When Bro would get uo in the morning, I wasn't able to fall back to sleep, so I would go into the living room, lie on the couch, turn on the radio and listen to DJ Ernie Simon Show on WJJD AM {we didn't have FM yet}. My mother always listened whenever she could.

One of my earliest memories of music was one New Year's Day when we went to visit my Aunt Eve and Uncle Junior. MY uncle was playing "Jambalaya" by Hank Williams Sr. on the phonograph. He was a huge fan of Hank's. As usual, my uncle was drinking. My father asked him what was wrong this time. My uncle replied, "Hank Williams died yesterday." That's all I really remember. I had heard of Hank Williams but never saw him then.

Around 1956 a new sound in music came into being. It was called "Rock N' Roll." At the same time came "Rock-A-Billy." It was Country and Western stars blending country music with rock n' roll. Stars like Johnny Cash, Elvis Presley, Roy Orbison and Jerry Lee Lewis to name a few. A lot of TV shows were geared to Country music. When we got a TV set we were able to actually see who was singing the music, it was neat. We saw stars like Eddy Arnold, Patsy Cline, Roy Acuff and many more. The "Barn Dance" and "ozark Jubilee" were some of the top shows. Later, the transistor radio came out. You didn't have to plug it in. It ran on batteries and you could put it in your pocket and listen to it wherever you went.

Buddy Holley was one of the hottest, brightest, youngest stars to hit the music charts. His style was like no one ever heard before or since. He had this hic-up voice that no one could copy successfully. He was every part of the word "sensation." This teen idol got Rock n Roll back to Rock n Roll. and people were dancing to his tunes world wide.

On the morning of February 4, 1959 I got out of bed and went into the kitchen to read the paper. The radio was playing "Everyday" by Buddy Holley. When the song was over Ernie Simon said, "That was 'Everyday' by the late Buddy Holley." I thought to myself, "What's he talking about?" My mother handed me the paper and it read, "Buddy Holley and three other's die in plane crash." Just 21 years old..dead, along with 17 yr. old Richie Valens and 22 yr. old J.P. Richardson, a.k.a. "The Big Bopper." The first real tragedy of it's kind. Within 2 weeks the air-waves were playing songs of tragedy about young lovers, teenagers, break-ups. Music was changed forever. Music now was ballads, Doo-Wop etc. Folk music became popular for years. Country music out sold Rock n Roll. When Buddy Holley died so did the music, and so did a part of America.

CHAPTER TWELVE

CHRISTMAS AT OUR

HOUSE

XMAS AT OUR HOUSE

ME - 4 YEARS OLD

CHRISTMAS AT OUR HOUSE

As I think about Christmas's past while growing up I can now realize how special they really were. As kids growing up in the 1950's, we never had much of an idea how really poor we were or even knowing what the word "Poor" really meant. In fact, when saying, 'You poor thing," we really didn't know what we were even talking about because we picked it up from someone who was saying it, so we'd say it.

As far as material things, we considered getting one toy a real luxury. We couldn't wait till next year to get another one, then we'd have two of them. We mostly got clothes from Aunts and Uncles-boring. One toy had to last because there was no such thing as a replacement.

Christmas Eve was more special. Around 17 people would somehow squeeze in at our house and everyone would bring something to eat. There was always something for everyone. It was cozy, fun, and real homey. Most of the people were gone by 10 pm. My Uncle Joe and my Dad would sit around having a beer or two. My mother, sister, brother and me would join my Aunt Katie and her daughter, my cousin, "Cookie," for midnight mass. We always had plenty of snow for Christmas. The sky would be clear enough to see the moon {sometimes full} and stars. The lady who lived three doors down had an outside speaker and play "Silent Night." We could hear it as we approached the car. It was so beautiful. You could almost cry. I wish I could hear that one more time.

When we came back from mass we would turn on the TV and watch "A Christmas Carol." After that was over we would leave Santa some milk and cookies. In the morning when we got up we could see that Santa doesn't clean up after himself. He always left crumbs, never did dishes, and never finished his milk. What a slob.

As we got a little older my brother and I were getting curious as to why we were always told to "Stay out of the closet." One early Christmas Eve both parents had to go out. Bro and I decided to see just what the fuss was all about. We went to see for ourselves. When we looked in there we saw many presents, some with my name on them. I was very excited. Bro showed no emotion. Little did I know that tomorrow a couple of bombs would drop. Bomb #1: Those gifts in the closet were the only ones under the tree. No toys, just clothes. Santa wasn't coming. I thought that I was good most of the year. MY sister was the only one getting toys. Sheee's the "baby" of the family, that's why. There should have been at least one for me anyway. I asked myself, self! "Did Santa forget me? Or just skip us?" He must have been on strike. Who needs clothes? We already have some. I did get a Duane Eddy record at least.

But that wasn't the last of it. Bomb #2 was about ready to drop.

My sister was told to go upstairs and get dressed. My mother, father and brother sat with me in the living room by the tree. They told me in a soft voice that "There really is no Santa Claus." Man, oh, man! What a pits for a Christmas. First no toys, just clothes, and now , no Santa Claus? That's why there wasn't any toys. Also, I found out that my brother and my parents conspired to have Bro take me into the closet. Bro knew all that time. Traumatic! to say the least. all at once, at age 13. What could I say?

The following Christmas wasn't any better; I asked my father, "When are we going to put up the tree?" I loved that piney smell of fresh Christmas trees. We always get it from the place on the corner of Washington Blvd. and Bohland Ave. next to the tavern. My father said he'd bring it home "Tomorrow." The next day he came home carrying two boxes. I asked him what was in the boxes and he replied, "The tree." "What?" I said, "How do you get a tree in a box?" I thought. We all gathered in the living room to see this. When he opened the box we were shocked and disappointed. It was artificial, silver aluminum tree that you had to put together. Not only that, you decorated it with red ornaments. A color wheel would turn around displaying three different colors. EEEEK!

Christmas was never the same after that. My mother would die two months later. The days of midnight mass ' was over and, as for the music outside, never to be heard again. The people sold the house and moved away. We even had to pray just to get a little snow for Christmas. Those early days of Christmas, well, they were the best ever, unforgettable.

X-MAS AT OUR HOUSE

XMAS TREE 1956

X-MAS AT OUR HOUSE

ME AND DIANE XMAS 1964

XMAS AT OUR HOUSE

UNCLE JOHN - BUTCH-{ BACK]
ME - DIANNA 12-25-1950

L- R- BUTCH & ME
DEC. 25, 1951

EPILOGUE

Well! There you have it as well as I could remember. You have met some of the people that were an important part of my life during those years. All the people and incidents were all a part of growing up in a small town called Bellwood, Illinois.

I have no regrets as life wasn't easy nor was it all that hard either. Whether these people remember me or not is not important to me..I remember them and can thank them for being a huge part of my life.

A lot of things have changed since then. Some of the businesses are gone or the buildings are taken over by new ones. All the homes remain but have new tenants with kids making new memories.

It's been a long time, lots of things to remember, good times, bad times, good neighbors, crabby neighbors... they were all a part of it.

I miss my old home town and the people that were in it. I will always have a place in my heart for Bellwood, Il. and will always remember "The days gone by.

GRANDPARENTS

ELIZABETH   *GOTTLIEB*

ALTENHOFF FAMILY

STANDING L - R AUNT ESTHER DAD AUNT MARY
SEATED L - R AUNT BETTY GRANDMA & GRANDPA

FAMILY ALBUM
ALL FIVE OF US

ME   DAD   DIANNA   MOM   BUTCH

ME   MOM   DAD   DIANNA   BUTCH

MY MOTHER-HELEN

**MOTHER & MY GRANDMA
YORCIS - 1942**

MY MOTHER-HELEN

MOMS' GRADUATION
MAY 30, 1940

ME AGE FIVE -1

ME AGE FIVE -2

IN MEMORIAM
IN LOVING MEMORY OF MY LATE SISTER
DIANNA ALTENHOFF LaCOCO
JULY 15, 1949 - OCT. 18, 2006
SHE WAS SO MUCH A PART OF MY LIFE AND WITH

HER ENCOURAGEMENT I WROTE THIS BOOK

ABOUT THE AUTHOR

About the author? I was going to delete this because this book is about the author and most of you already know who I am but didn't know me back then, so there, I'm glad that I cleared that up. This is a fun trip through the 1950's and I hope you enjoy it. This book is factual and is told exactly the way i remember it. Based on my memory, some stories are long and some are short. I always tell things "the way it is," straight forward.....You can believe it or not, but have fun and just go with it.